Don't Go!
A Practical Guide for Tackling Employee Turnover

Vernon H. Mason, Jr., MEd

ISBN-10: 1517476208
ISBN-13: 978-1517476205

DEDICATION

With a $5,000 credit card in 1991, my mother and I opened a small child care center with a capacity of 30 children. She worked in the Nursery for a few years and I cooked and often "supervised" the Pre-K room in late afternoons. My mother was wonderful with the children. She taught me through her actions that children want to be loved, respected and have fun. She knew intuitively that if we did those three things, then we would be successful! She also taught me the important point that "they are our paycheck." This book is dedicated to my mother.

CONTENTS

Acknowledgments

It is hard to believe that some form of this book has been in development for 30 years. Almost every job I have ever had I have always been handed or worked myself up into a supervisory role. Even when I was in high school working in fast food I was offered the weekend manager's job. I was only 17 years old and the location was in a somewhat marginal area of town, so I decided to decline the offer. I then went to work at the local movie theater and quickly found myself again a key carrier with opening and closing responsibilities. I learned early on that the employees you supervise can make you or break you. It is something of an art to find the right balance of compassion, empathy, sympathy, and a firm hand.

These acknowledgments would be incomplete if I did not mention the dedicated, hardworking employees I have had over the years who have seen me at my best and my worst. My longest-employed staff member is Ms. Susan D., the best substitute in the world! There are countless others, and if I tried to name them all I would surely forget someone. So, I will just say THANK YOU from the bottom of my heart. You are the wind beneath my wings, and without your commitment, hard work, and dedication I would have never survived this journey! Many of you have become life-long friends and family, like Marcia, my longtime assistant director. I say she will always be a friend because "she knows where the bodies are buried" (just kidding).

To my peers, and especially the ones I have quoted and/or used in my examples, I say thank you! You make me strive to become better.

A great thanks goes to my editor, G. Sherman H. Morrison, who held my hand through this process and even added some valuable content.

My gratitude goes out to my many mentors, such as Rashmi Nakhre, Becky Bailey, and Paula Jorde Bloom. Thank you!

I have to especially thank my business coach and friend Kris Murray for her persistence and inspiration in pushing me to write this book. Kris, you amaze me, and your touching Foreword means the world to me!

I met Holly Elissa Bruno may years ago and I felt an immediate kindred spirit. She co-taught with Gwen Morgan a college course I took while I was working on my master's degree. What a dynamic duo! I so appreciate Holly's writing a foreword for this book and being such a force of nature. I strive every day to be as open, as free, and as loving as she is!

To live a full and happy life you have to have great friends, so I must mention a few of my stress-relievers, venting partners, and judgment-free friends, such as Windell, Mike, Robin, Rocky, Johnny, Dee Dee, Tracey, Susan B. and my cousin Kim. My great friend Tiffany, thanks for letting me bend your ear, keeping me grounded and your valuable input.

To my family: I especially appreciate your unconditional acceptance. I am grateful to my family, starting back with my father's parents who were hard-working commercial fisherman and somehow seemed to save almost more than they made. To my mother's parents, who worked night and day on the farm, I am thankful for inheriting their strong work ethic. I am also thankful to my dad from whom I get my calmness and my mom from whom I get my sense of humor.

To my partner in life: Andy, you have been on this journey making me laugh the whole way. Thanks for your patience, and for having confidence in me even when we had to put it all on the line.

I'll finish with a line I use in one of my keynote addresses: "Nobody said it would be easy, but it will be worth it."

Vernon Mason

Foreword(s)

Do you know someone who always makes you smile? He may be crazy, but when you see him coming down the street, you will cross the street to walk beside him?

Vernon is that person for me. Vernon is an optimist. He can't stop believing that early childhood professionals are invaluable. He can't be persuaded that any of us is that "glorified babysitter" we hear we are. He refuses to believe our best teachers will inevitably leave us behind. He's convinced he can resolve the staff retention problem.

Vernon is out to prove the naysayers wrong. If you have lost hope about retaining your best teachers, you might need a dose of *Don't Go!*

Vernon has a unique way of transforming something impossible into something do-able while adding a dollop of humor along the way. He's been in the business for 24 years and has ample tips to share. Which is exactly what he has taken on as his task: How to keep our best teachers when we:

- Can't pay them enough.
- Can't reward them enough.
- Can't compete with public schools.
- Can't change the condescending perspective on our unsung profession.

When Vernon says "Don't go," he also says, "I need you. The children need you. Our profession needs you. And I'll do everything in my power to make this a school you simply cannot leave."

So can anyone, even an incurable optimist like Vernon, resolve the seemingly unresolvable? That's for you to decide.

I have decided. Vernon's honest, transparent, loving and no-nonsense approach to retaining the best teachers works. In his years as a director he proved it could be done.

Hey, you have nothing to lose but pessimism. Give this book a chance. Even if it helps you retain one teacher, you'll discover this book has paid for itself.

Oh, did I tell you Vernon's office consists of glass walls? Transparency is his style. He holds nothing back and offers you all he has. And what he has might just be something you could use.

Kick jadedness to the curb. Take a stroll with Vernon. See what you can discover about making your program a solid, mature, and dynamic organization where year after year, children and their families can count on you for the best of everything, especially the most loving, expert, and seasoned teachers.

~ Holly Elissa Bruno ~ October, 2015

Holly Elissa Bruno is a best-selling author, international keynoter, and radio host. Her most recent book, *The Comfort of Little Things: An Educator's Guide to Second Chances* (Redleaf, 2015) received the Living Now Silver Book Award for books that "improve our quality of life."

I've known Vernon Mason for about five years now. If you haven't had the pleasure of meeting Vernon or seeing him speak at an early childhood conference, allow me the guilty pleasure of telling you a little bit about the man.

Vernon is one of those rare human beings who was put on this planet to make us feel happy, loved, and if we deserve it, respected. He is a *very* funny man. Open-minded, open-hearted, and a great leader. I'm so glad he has written this book. Vernon chose to carry forward his mother's legacy of high-quality child care, and he has seen great success. I attribute his success to the positive culture he has created in his schools, and his thoughtful yet "no BS" leadership style. A style much like my own. No wonder I love the guy.

A few years ago, Vernon declared that he was finally going to finish this book. I strongly encouraged him to do so, and as his business coach would consistently ask him, "So how's the book coming along?" I am so proud of him for finishing this excellent resource that will be used by many to make their early childhood programs stronger and more stable.

Running a child care business can be very difficult and challenging, let alone the effort it takes to make your program successful and profitable. It's been said that staff turnover rates in our industry hover around 35 percent annually. This means three or four teachers out of every ten you hire will leave you within one year. That's a lot of churn and expense, not to mention time and headaches. I promise that if you read this book and embrace its ideas and strategies, your turnover will decline and your teacher happiness will increase. It's a bold statement, but Vernon Mason is a master of this topic. Quite simply, he's one of the best leaders I know, and a true expert in the areas of team motivation, staff retention, and outside-the-box leadership.

Happy reading! ~ Kris Murray ~ September, 2015

Chapter 1: Tackling Turnover

First things first: FIRE SOMEONE!

I know, it seems odd to start out a book about reducing your turnover with the phrase "Fire someone." This book came from a workshop I have been doing for several years called *Tackling Turnover.* Just as I was about to complete it, a new title came to me: "Don't Go!" Over the years, every time I would do the *Tackling Turnover* workshop, many directors' take-away would be "I have to go back and fire Negative Nellie." Many of us go into the field of early childhood education and childcare because we enjoy watching children grow and learn. They are so precious, innocent and fun (well, most of the time!) We did not go into early childhood to supervise staff, chase down tuition, and engage in the always-fun balancing a budget (i.e., keeping the lights on!) The most challenging of the three, I would say, is the staff supervision and the inevitable human resource challenges the will come along. Because of the loving, nurturing personalities we have, we are typically not of the aggressive, confrontational types of supervisors. With the transition from working with children to supervising adults come the following bad practices that represent the easy way out in the short-term but are more difficult in the long-term, and actually wind up making your good staff leave:

1. We often become friends with staff and can't transition into being their supervisors. We believe if they like us enough they will do what we want.

2. Supervising by not supervising. We believe if we ignore the situation it will take care of itself or work itself out.

3. We'll address it with the whole group because we believe it is rude or inappropriate for us to address our concerns directly with individual staff members.

4. Some directors are intimidated by strong-willed staff members.

5. If I make them mad, they will leave.

In reality, these practices and beliefs make our turnover *worse* and often set us up to inadvertently reward and give perceived authority to the negative staff. I remember years ago when my assistant director and I were challenging the significant negative "click" we somehow had managed to develop. Sometimes it only takes one bad seed and it can take root before you realize it has done so. We addressed the situation and terminated the "ring leader." It was tough because, of course, these were for the most part staff members that the parents really enjoyed.

Sometimes the staff the parents like most are the worst employees. Often the staff that parents like aren't that good with their children and the staff the parents don't like are quite good with their children. That is a subject I need to work on for another book!

In my *Tackling Turnover* workshop, I talk about how the negative staff or the weak links we keep on staff actually makes the job of our good and great employees that much harder. Bad employees going unchecked is often the reason good employees leave. A couple years ago, I read a phrase that was very enlightening. It went something like this: *Who knows who the weak or bad employees are? The good employees. Who has to work harder to take up the slack for a weak employee? The good employees.*

Do you have an employee that needs a little reigning in? Do you have an employee who has gone completely unchecked? Is it time to protect your great staff? I don't say this lightly, but if you have done all you can do (within reason), then it is time to take action, and your first step in tackling turnover may be firing someone!

What is Your Turnover Rate?

There are advanced, elaborate, detailed methods for calculating your turnover rate, but the simplest way of a quick calculation comes from Gerry Pastor at Educational Playcare in Connecticut. He suggests taking your w-2s for the year, dividing them by the number of positions you have, then subtracting 1 from that. Example: You have 85 w-2s and you have 50 positions. I know you're going to groan, but put the book down and go get last year's W9s and W2s and calculate:

# of positions/divided by # of W2's – Minus 1 = Turnover rate

_____ / _____ — 1 = _____

How do you compare to others? I have found a great user-friendly site to show you turnover rates: http://www.talx.com/benchmarks/turnover/index.asp.

Once you know your turnover rate, then what? Are you surprised? Information is power! *Nothing will change unless something changes.* Now you have your starting point.

Mindset is important. We must understand that employees work for more than just a paycheck. Supervisors will say they should just do it because it is their job, so why should they have to praise them and thank them? The answer is surprisingly simple: Lots of research efforts confirm that a happier workforce is more productive!

It has been said that buying doughnuts and leaving them in the lounge will not improve your turnover. That is a true statement. But what I believe and have learned in practice over the years is that something as simple as buying doughnuts and taking them around *personally* while interacting with each staff member *will* help improve and build your relationship with your staff. In writing this book, I kept in mind the following two facts:

1. Directors are doers and prefer lists, directions and/or a roadmap.

2. Directors also have limited time and budgets.

This book is full of my best practices I have used or picked up from other directors over the years. No one activity in this book will make everything perfect. It is the effort you put into improving your staff morale that will be seen and felt by your staff and ultimately improve (reduce) your turnover. I recommend you take this book in chunks and select easier activities to accomplish and then continue moving through to the more difficult practices.

There are so many professional development books out there for business leaders concerning workplace environments. I have read almost all of them. They each have a similar yet slightly differ twist on what employees want from their supervisors. I absorbed their ideas and have come up with my own list. I call it the *Director's Pledge*. The list is a concrete reminder of what I believe your employees want from their supervisors. Check it out on the next page:

Directors Pledge

1. **I will set clear expectations** while regularly giving feedback and encouraging development by offering opportunities to learn and grow.
   a. I will train employees until they feel competent.
2. I will ensure that my staff have the **materials and equipment** needed to do the job right.
3. **I will compliment more than I complain**: I will regularly, publicly praise staff for doing good work. I will also know and openly appreciate staff strengths.
4. I will ask for, genuinely listen to, and learn from **staff opinions**.
5. I will share an **accurate and current mission/purpose** of our company/center to ensure my staff of the **importance** of their jobs.
6. I will only **employ staff who are committed to doing quality work** to ensure my staff only works with other dedicated, committed people.
7. **I will find reasons to celebrate**, play, and have fun together.
   a. I will find some way to make their day.
8. **I will be the example.**
   a. I will remain optimistic and expect the best, remembering that I am judged during difficult times, that my reputation will be built during the difficult times, and remembering my staff needs to be hopeful.
   b. I will be trustworthy, letting my word be golden and never betraying confidences.

    c. I will pay attention, be present, and will be nice to my staff, showing empathy for the jobs they do.

9. I will **implement a reward system** so that my staff experience a tangible method of appreciation.

10. I will **regularly interact** with my staff and **build positive relationships.** I will encourage an environment of relationship-building at work.

11. **Before criticizing**, I will assume what Carol Gateway says: "When someone does something wrong, I will first assume it is a training or policy problem."

What Can We do to Reduce Turnover?

Track it! That's why I had you calculate a baseline Turnover Rate a few pages ago. Why is this important? The following quote provides the answer:

"What gets measured improves." ~ Kris Murray

You must also learn to acknowledge the truth of why people leave, about which I'll have more to say later on.

Ad Writing Exercise

These days, hiring is a lot like being in sales! To gain insight **write a job ad** for a prospective employee in which you describe your characteristics as a "boss," say something about your management traits or style, and so on. To get a feel for what I'm after with this exercise, trying addressing the following ideas in your ad:

    I will lead you by….

    I will support you by….

    You can count on me for….

Use the space on the next page to write up your job ad:

JOB AD

Now think about the following:

> What would your ad look like if your employees wrote it?

> What traits or characteristics would they point out?

> What would they say are your strengths?

> What would they say are your weakness?

Remember: Perception is reality!

Could you work for yourself? Honestly…no excuses! With hindsight being 20/20, have you lost staff that you wish you had done more to save?

You're a BANKER!

Staff retention and relationship building is like each staff member having a bank account, and you're in charge of it! This is an analogy; it has nothing to do with pay.

Every interaction you have with an employee is a deposit or withdrawal.

Our best employees should have the highest balances. We must have some staff whose accounts are so high they can take a few withdrawals and still be in the positive.

Deposits: These are the positive interactions that you have with the employee, not typically formal interactions like a conference or performance appraisals. These are the everyday, positive feelings and interactions the employee gets from you, other administrators, other employees, and customers.

Then there are all the items that take away from the deposits you make. These are things that happen when an employees has to come to work and deal with un-fun things like vomiting children, late coworkers, negative coworkers, weak coworkers, disconnected supervisors, a supervisor that only speaks to them when complaining, and so on.

- **Writing a Check:** Change of work hours they don't like.

- **A Monthly Draft:** Getting training outside of work hours.

- **Withdrawal:** Negative feedback, but if constructive then not so bad.

- **Overdrawn:** You've gone too far with negative feedback.

- **Continually Over Drawn:** Your feedback is always negative.

How are your accounts? Who is overdrawn? It should only be your weakest staff member. Are all your accounts overdrawn? You better start making some deposits.

Another analogy is that building up employees is kind of like a parking meter. To show ongoing appreciation, you have to keep depositing so the time does not expire.

Why do Employees Leave?

- What do you think are the reasons employee's leave?
- Do the supervisors and employee's agree on why they left?
- Write down right now the last 10 employees that left.
- Write beside their names *why* they left.

WHY DID THEY LEAVE?

1. _____

2. _____

3. _____

4. _____

5. _____

6. _____

7. _____

8. _____

9. _____

10. _____

Did they tell you the truth? I know I often will find out the truth from other employees or parents about why someone left.

Supervision by Inaction!

I believe this is why often the "good" employee leaves and we are left with the less desirable or at times the "bad" employee.

Protect Your Staff!

Scientific studies show that attitudes are **contagious**! Consider the following:

- After just 15 minutes of interaction your physiology, heart rate, blood pressure, skin temperature, etc. become aligned with one another (from the book *Hug Your People*, 2008)

- A Harvard study on happiness proves that it is contagious…like a virus spreading!

So why do the good ones leave?

Chapter 2: Relationship-Building with Staff

I closed the last chapter with the all-important question: Why do the good ones leave? It's really important for you to understand the following point:

People leave <u>managers</u>, NOT <u>companies</u>!

Plenty of studies prove that people leave managers, not companies. You might have the same companies, same benefits, same leave time, salaries, etc., and yet turnover rates can be dramatically different between pretty equal setups. It all comes down to the managers.

"As a manager, you only have one thing to invest: your time."

Laws of Teamwork, by John C. Maxwell

Maxwell understands that when it comes to time, it's about with *whom* you spend it, and *how* you spend it with them. That's what really determines your success as a manager.

No matter what your occupation, be it as a doctor, psychiatrist, marriage counselor, preacher, lawyer, or anything else. The key is that you have to *give of yourself.*

We all want to belong!

Research shows that it is a fundamental desire to "belong." We have a basic human desire for interpersonal attachments (see "The

Need to Belong" by R. F. Baumeister and M. R. Leary in *Psychological Bulletin*, volume 117, number 3, 1995, pages 497-529).

It's all about Relationships

A strong relationship begins with TRUST. But TRUST is fragile, being much easier to lose than create. As investment guru Warren Buffet says, "Trust is like the air we breathe. When it's present, nobody really notices. But when it's absent, everybody notices."

My own definition of trust is: *Following through on what you say or promise.* If you can't follow through, then you owe them an explanation.

No SURPRISES unless they are positive!

- Most of the time the unknown is often worse than reality.
- This ranges from small things like "am I getting off work on time?"
- To bigger areas like employees not finding out until receiving a performance appraisal that you are unhappy with their work.

Know something about your TEAM!

- Names, children's names.
- Employee's interests.
- What's going on in their lives?
- Everybody has a story.
- Your curiosity shows you care!
- Also, always be sure to spell employees' names correctly!

CBWA: Caring by Walking Around

Pay attention to what they're doing and how they're feeling. And always be genuine...they can smell a fraud from a mile away! Words and body language should match deeds. Enthusiasm is required, and all of this is great for quality control.

There has been a concept for years called "supervising by walking around." The concept of *caring by walking around* is another take on that concept. I believe that a good director, manager, or administrator cannot do a great job by sitting in their office.

Office hermits, as I call them, are often disconnected from what is really happening throughout the organization. I can assure you they are the first to respond to an email and can tell you exactly who is saying what on Facebook. When you want to go from *good* to *great*, your first step is to get out of your office! Mingle with the employees and you will most of the time see the problems coming and either head them off or know what needs to be done to make a quick and effective course correction.

Caring by walking around is not difficult, especially considering what it in and of itself will do for morale. It is easily one of the best uses of your time. It breaks the walls down between you and your staff. It is as basic as speaking to staff members, and then they will mostly take it from there. Many supervisors resist this concept because of the following two reasons:

The number one reason is the time it takes. I do not believe you have to do this every single day. When I was a director of a large childcare program, I would make my way around once or twice each week. I think that can be sufficient. I believe the *quality* of the interaction is more important than the *quantity* or how often it happens. Now, having said that, I also believe you should make your way around at least once per week. Other options would be to take turns with another administrator. Also, sometimes staff may say something to one administrator they would not say to another. This can be due to history, comfort level, or a trust issue, so keep that in mind.

The Number 2 reason why administrators resist this concept is because they want to avoid negative staff. You know there's always at least one who never has anything nice to say, always has a complaint, and rarely is anything done right or in a way that suits them. I have the following three recommendations about negative staff:

1. If you don't like interacting with negative staff, what do you think your other staff members think of them? How is she influencing other staff? I can assure you it is not in a positive way!

2. Don't engage with Negative Nellie. Make a statement like "I know you're going to have an awesome day," or try, "It is just beautiful outside today," or even, "It's a great day! I don't know how anyone could complain today."

3. Another option is from Kris, who is my friend, coach, and guru of ALL things related to childcare marketing (check out her website at http://childcare-marketing.com.) She says ask them this: "What's new and good today?" If someone cannot respond positively to that on most days, you really need to consider if they should be working for you.

Treat Them like Someone Special!

- Treat staff extra special on holidays
- This can be as simple as a card, candy, flowers, or lunch

One Valentine's Day I was on my way to work. I stopped at a big box store and they had their roses on sale at half-price. I purchased enough so that I could wrap a single rose in tissue. I walked around and handed them out to the staff. Of course everyone said thank you, but the real payoff came the next day. I had one staff member tell me they really appreciated the rose because I was the only adult who had given her anything on Valentine's Day. Sometimes the little things are the best things!

When I think of what to do on a holiday, I recommend avoiding junk food, especially on days the staff probably already has an abundance of it brought in by others. Sure, you can go big and have a great lunch catered in or even buy the staff all a pricey gift, but the important aspect is to acknowledge the day.

Hardships

- Encourage staff to pull together during these times.
- Plan to attend funerals of your staff's family members when they occur.
- Visit them in the hospital during times of sickness.
- Take a meal to the family sponsored by you or entire staff.

If you don't cook, then buy the ingredients and ask your cook to prepare a meal. Another option is get a frozen lasagna, bag of salad, and loaf of French or Italian bread from the grocery store. Trust me, it will be hugely appreciated!

When we supervise employees we always say leave your personal problems at the door. But there are times when that is simply not possible. When an employee has a significant hardship, it is a time we must at least minimally acknowledge what's happening in their life and that we understand what they're going through.

Many people will say, "I don't know what to say." I always recommend you keep it basic and say something like, "I am so sorry, is there anything I can do for you?" This is another area where what you do is not so important. What's more important is acknowledging an employee during their time of need or sorrow.

It is vital that someone from your leadership team attends funerals in person to pay their respects. I was the director of a large facility with 48 staff members. When you supervise that many staff, "hardships" are a regular occurrence. I worked with my administrative team and we devised a plan to take turns. One of us always attended, and we would make a point to say, "Ms. Sally said to tell you she sends her thoughts and prayers. She wishes she could have been here but she couldn't get out of her obligations tonight." They would say the same thing for me if I could not attend. It is also important to be consistent with the manner of acknowledgement, so I recommend you have a written guide to which administration can refer. Ours was something like this:

- Always pass a sympathy card around for the staff to sign.

- If the death was a spouse or child of an employee, we would attend the visiting hours, send flowers ($75 to $100), and provide a meal.

- If the death was a parent of an employee, we would attend the visiting hours and send flowers ($50).

- For other deaths in the family that met our bereavement policy, we would send flowers ($30).

What you do not want to happen is have someone undergo a significant hardship and have no one show up or acknowledges it in any way. That sends a very clear message, and not the message we want to send. Being visible and sending flowers builds relationships with not just your employees but also with their families. It maybe taboo to mention, but it is also good for PR and marketing.

I Heard Someone Say, "You Are What You Give"

I thought that was a thought provoking phrase. My interpretation of it is that when we show compassion then we are compassionate. The same thing goes for empathy, sympathy, pride, appreciation – I could go on and on. In reverse, the same thing can be said. We can give anger, uncaring, contempt, disrespect, snide remarks, belittling, and so on. If that's what you give, that's what you are. The problem is we are judged on how we respond during difficult times, not during the good days! Who can't be on their best behavior when everything is going well? The challenge is to understand an employee's perceptions. How does it look from *their* point of view?

Give what you want to be!

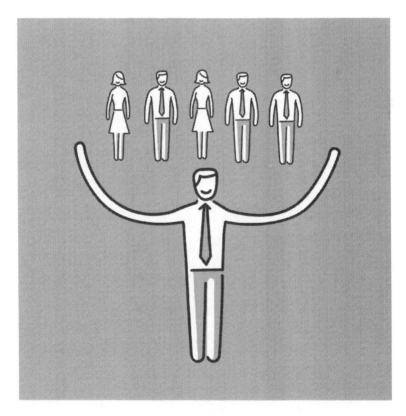

Chapter 3: Have FUN!

It should come as no surprise that *Have Fun* fits perfectly alongside *Relationship-Building with Staff.* In *Learn to be an Optimist* by Lucy MacDonald (2004), we learn some interesting things from studies on Laughter:

- Show muscles loosen up, heart rate and blood pressure are lowered, leaving you feeling relaxed, calm and positive.
- Laughter also boost immune system by increasing your level of T-cells, these defend you against infection

As it turns out, people are much more productive when they are having fun! So loosen up and have fun. Ah, but that's easier said than done, isn't it? I know that the responsibility that comes along with being in charge can be stressful, but we must learn to lighten up and laugh a little. Who on your staff makes you laugh? Go find them and get a good laugh. You will feel better and so will the people you supervise!

Share the FUN!

- Laughter can be the best medicine
- Post a joke or funny email
- Have you seen a funny story or picture on Facebook? Print it and post it in the staff lounge or restroom. Your staff will enjoy the laughter!

Kids are Funny!

Coming from the childcare industry, I can tell you with confidence that kids really do say and do the darndest things! Retell what you observe and it'll always get you a few good laughs, for yourself and others. Encourage your staff to bring a funny story to your next staff meeting. Let the staff vote and give a prize to the best story. Would it not be awesome to have your staff talking about how funny the children are instead of the children's negative behavior? Remember: what Becky Bailey says: Whatever you focus on most is exactly what you will get more of!

It's All About the FOOD

I started out the practice of *covered dish lunches* (what others might call potlucks) rather sporadically, but then it became more routine. Let me tell you, there is nothing better than surprising your staff with breakfast, lunch, or even a snack. I took the concept of feeding my staff to the next step of involving them, and actually made it into a teambuilding exercise. Depending on the level of enthusiasm and participation, your role will vary. I believe the lower your morale the more the leader has to do. Conversely, the higher the morale the less the leader has to do.

In the childcare field we never have a time when the entire staff can lunch together. I developed a pattern where right before the first staff went to lunch the second staff would come to the fix their plate and go back to eat while they were supervising naptime.

I found you cannot leave this sort of thing completely up to chance, so we developed a simple sign up form to indicate who is bringing what. I didn't like leaving anything to chance, so over time our sign up sheets became more and more involved. They have sign up blanks for specific categories. For example we would have 4 blanks for meats, 6 blanks for vegetables, 2 blanks for starches, 4 blanks for desserts and 6 blanks for drinks.

If I noticed my staff participation slacking off for the covered dish lunches, I would provide the meats and the staff would bring everything else. It just served to give a few of the people a break from feeling pressured to bring stuff in. And be sure to have these soon after a payday so the staff have money to participate!

Take it a Step Further

Create themes, add table decorations and colorful table cloths to show some enthusiasm. Get staff excited by sponsoring contests, such as the following:

- Chili Cook-Offs
- Best Desserts
- Cookie Bake-Off
- Snack Attack!
- Crock Pot Meals
- You're only limited by your imagination!

Celebrations

Employee Birthdays

- Send around cards to be signed by entire staff.
- If possible, give small gifts such as flowers or gift certificates.
- How about a day off with or without pay?
- Banners for momentous birthdays.
- Send a personal note from you.
- Equal treatment for all when it comes to birthdays!

Every organization has different abilities. Some cannot afford to give a day off with pay, or have the staff to cover that many days off. Some may not even afford flowers, but everyone can afford cards!

Equal treatment is something you must keep an eye out for. I have witnessed staff going all out for a popular staff member and then doing little or nothing for a staff member that was not popular. It has to be all or nothing, and as the supervisor you must be very clear and direct in handling this.

- Plan baby or wedding showers for staff, or better yet, have your Committee plan them. Delegation is a beautiful thing.

- Sponsor lunches to acknowledge an employee's completion of a degree, certificate, classes, etc.

- If invited, attend special occasions, family celebrations of the staff, etc.

Don't Wait to Celebrate

There are so many different things besides holidays that all represent opportunities to celebrate. In the childcare/daycare setting, I always make sure we take advantage of the following:

- High enrollment
- Fund raising efforts
- Re-licensing, accreditation, Environment Rated Scales results
- Staff attendance
- Lack of turnover
- School starting back

And pretty much anytime I feel my staff needs a little boost, I make sure to feed them, whether it's an ice cream party, a nice selection of fresh fruit, homemade smoothies, or fresh-cooked omelets. Never underestimate the power of food to raise morale!

Whatever the occasion for fun, the important aspect of this is for *you* as a supervisor/director to be involved in the activities. This not about sending your cook around with ice cream bars; it is about *you* interacting and showing first-hand your appreciation for your staff.

Chapter 4: Encouragement

Back in Chapter 1 I quoted Kris Murray, who says, "What gets measured improves." That's her take on a similar quote, although I haven't been able to figure out who said it. It goes like this: *What gets measured, gets done. What gets rewarded, gets done well.* What this means is that you need to specifically **budget for retention activities!**

"When you do good, you feel good-when you feel good, you do good."

Laws of Teamwork, by John C. Maxwell

Encouragement

- Research shows "performance is higher when people were led by individuals who gave more encouragement." Kouzes and Posner, c.1995
- 98% of people say they perform better when encouraged.
- Building Up and Climbing Higher!
- You do need to document until you create a pattern. Also helps keep it consistent.

Think about how you perform best. I'd be willing to bet that, like most people, you perform better with encouragement and praise. I'd be surprised to hear of anyone who performs best when being ignored, reprimanded, or threatened. The idea is very simple – people need *encouragement* to be peak performers.

As supervisors and directors, most of us need a reminder to praise our employees. I encourage you to document encouragement by tracking who and when you praise. This tracking will get you in the habit of showing encouragement evenly and on a regular basis. See the next page for a simple chart to make this happen:

Building Up and Climbing Higher!

Monday	Tuesday	Wednesday	Thursday	Friday
Date: Employee: Positive Reinforcement:	Date: Employee: Positive Reinforcement:	Date: Employee: Positive Reinforcement:	Date: Employee: Positive Reinforcement:	Date: Employee: Positive Reinforcement:
Date: Employee: Positive Reinforcement:	Date: Employee: Positive Reinforcement:	Date: Employee: Positive Reinforcement:	Date: Employee: Positive Reinforcement:	Date: Employee: Positive Reinforcement:
Date: Employee: Positive Reinforcement:	Date: Employee: Positive Reinforcement:	Date: Employee: Positive Reinforcement:	Date: Employee: Positive Reinforcement:	Date: Employee: Positive Reinforcement:

Pat Staff on the Back

- Hugs, actual pats on the back, or even take their hand. It's *powerful.*
- It's the cheapest form of praise because it *costs nothing.*
- It totally lifts the spirit of the *giver,* not just the *receiver!*
- The impact can be more powerful than saying "Thank you."

The cheapest and easiest way to show appreciation is to personally display it by taking a hand, giving a hug, or literally patting an employee on their back. You can gauge the personal space of each person so you don't take it too far and offend them in some way. You can also just ask them, "Are you a hugger?" They will tell you, and then you'll know if it's appropriate or not. If they or you are not huggers then take their hand in your hand and sandwich it with your other hand and say, "thank you."

Catch Them Doing Something RIGHT!

You'll remember that earlier I mentioned CBWA (caring by walking around). Now it's time for EBWA – encouraging by walking around.

- Catch them doing something right, mention it to them.
- Look for the positive.
- Remember: You mainly see what you look for.
- Enthusiasm is required.
- This is also great for quality control.

I have said for years that a good director cannot direct from an office. A great director must be visible and roam around the organization often to truly know what is going on in the classrooms and to positively interact and build a rapport with the staff. While you are roaming, of course you must address health and safety concerns, but your goal is to find employees doing something right!

Praise staff by acknowledging them in parent newsletters or staff memos. Find as many places as possible to praise your staff. Remember that whatever you focus on is what you will get more of!

Acknowledge Success

Long Term Staff

- Assign them a parking space!
- Celebrate work anniversaries: 10, 15, 20, etc.
- What else can you think of?

Above & Beyond "Bucks"

- Create fake money "bucks" for staff to earn.
- These "bucks" may be redeemed for extras such as hours/days off, prizes, or surprise gifts.
- Get ideas from staff as to what they would enjoy spending their "bucks" on.

With the fake money you can have an auction at a staff meeting or they can purchase from a menu from the company store.

Teacher of the Year

- Have staff vote on other staff based on their best qualities (not by popularity)
- Peer voting is more respected then being given by the administration which can be interpreted as rewarding their favorite.
- Best compliment is by one's peers, who view others as extraordinary

Many centers do a teacher of the month, but I believe the teacher of the year is more meaningful. When I have discussed the teacher of the month with centers, it almost seems as if it ends up just being rotated around in a "whose turn is it" kind of way, and that's no good because it doesn't stand for anything meaningful.

Whichever way you decide to award is fine, as long as it is done well and not selected by the administration. I like it to be peer-driven. What better compliment can you get than the people you work with everyday saying you are the best and deserve the recognition? A simple system can be put into place for the criteria. For example, must have been here for a certain length of time, cannot be the current holder of the title, and so on.

Make sure you budget for a reward to the teacher who wins. For years I gave a check for $75, $100, or $150 to the winner, and they were quite appreciative. A few years ago I decided to start asking for donations of $1 from parents and families attending our Christmas Program. We let the parents know in advance that the funds raised would all go to the Teacher of the Year award. Since starting this new practice, we have been able to give between $500 and $600 each year to the teacher of the year. Talk about appreciation!

We actually announce it the night of our Christmas Program so the parents can see the excitement and they all applaud for the teacher. It is one of the best win-win situations I've seen for building excitement with staff and families.

Years of Service

- Celebrate staff's years of service to the center.
- Plaques, cards, and lunches are ways to express gratitude for their loyalty.
- Great incentive for fundraising.
- Increase vacation time proportionately to time served (woops, I mean length of employment).

Parking

- Designate a prime slot with a visible sign acknowledging the staff member's award as "Teacher of the Year."
- Longevity Named/Reserved Parking.
- Follow up by issuing plaques, certificates, pins, or name badges honoring the winner(s).

Finding great new employees is a challenge, and it has been said that they are our second customer. Many of us spend almost as much time recruiting new employees as we do recruiting new customers. So when you get good ones that are long-term, we have to find ways to make them a part of us so the thought of leaving doesn't even seem like an option. What better way or more public way can you show your appreciation than to give them a dedicated parking space?

Chapter 5: Positive Interactions with Staff

As directors and supervisors, when we interact with our staff we have the following two choices:

1. Lift them up (building goodwill).

2. Push them down (expending goodwill).

I'm not just talking about job performance, I'm talking about *all* interactions in general, including passing in the hallways, coming in first thing in the morning, and so on.

Good Morning

Visit each room in the mornings to offer a "Good Morning" to the staff and the children at the start of the day.

When I was the opening administrator at my center it had been open about 30 minutes when I would arrive. I would come in, turn on the lamps, make my coffee, and then I would wander down the hall and speak to each class. The good thing was there were only three or four classes open at that point, so it wasn't very time consuming at all.

If you don't open your center and all the classrooms are open by the time you arrive, it takes a little longer but it is more than worth the reward. Those hugs and smiling faces will just totally brighten your day. Now, will the negative staff try to stop your groove and tell you everything that has gone wrong? Yes, and when that happens you have a couple options:

- #1 Stop her in her tracks and say, "We'll get to it later."
- #2 Respond with "Thanks for wanting to tell me, but I need you to write that down."
- #3 If she is genuinely negative every single day, then call her out on it. Say, "Sally, do you realize you have something negative to say every single day when I come in here? Tomorrow I want you to give me something positive."
- #4 is a reminder of what we covered in Chapter 2, Caring By Walking Around from Kris Murray, and she recommends you greet the negative staff by saying, "Tell me something new and good."

Spend Time With Your Staff

- Spend time during the day in the "employees' space."
- Have lunch in the staff lounge.

At all cost you must always avoid developing an atmosphere that it is *us against them…management against the workers…administration against classroom staff…center staff against the owner.* It's no good and poisons a center over time, making it completely dysfunctional.

This kind of atmosphere just drains the morale of the staff. As a supervisor, you want to be approachable and appear warm and friendly. In some ways, being a good supervisor is like being a politician. You smile and wave, listen to problems, and kiss a lot of babies. This concept is different from *Caring by Walking Around.* This is about you being in their space, where they hang out on their lunches. Have lunch in your staff lounge. Do they go in there in the mornings and drink coffee? Join them. This will keep that wall from building up. I'm *not* talking about gossiping with them. Most of the time you won't even talk about work, which is a good thing!

Lunch Bunch

- Gather groups together to dine at a nearby restaurant.
- Talk about topics other than work.
- Great tool in getting to know employees and their interests.

When I was a director, we had a pattern where a lot of staff would go to lunch at noon and then another set would go at 1:15. Once in a while, I would arrange my lunch so I was free at noon or 1:15 and when they were coming up the hall I would say, "I'm feeling like Mexican food, anyone want to join me?" The word would spread and we always would have anywhere from six to ten of us. We would laugh and they would talk and I would mostly just listen, taking it all in. There were times where it gave me insight about an employee, and there were also times I would learn more than I would want to know about some of them! I would rarely ever talk about work.

Directors have said "I can't have a relationship with staff that I supervise." I completely disagree, a healthy relationship makes employees care, and you cannot pay them enough to care. You can pay people to *work*, but you can't pay people to *care* and put in genuine effort.

My Definition of RELATIONSHIP

For our purposes, the term relationship means to be kind, caring, compassionate and developing an ongoing connection.

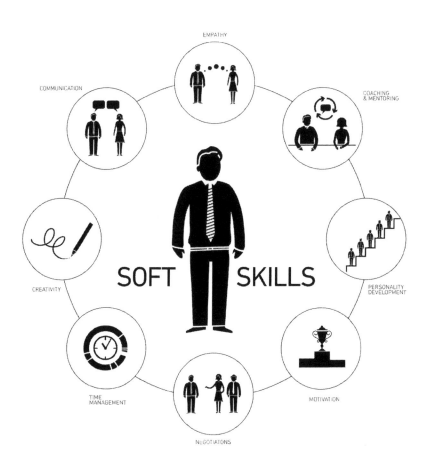

Chapter 6: Ongoing Communication

Staff Communication

- Provide a dry erase board in the staff lounge.
- Allows teachers to communicate with each other.
- Provides a way for peers to communicate praises/gripes.

You will be surprised how the staff will address things that you never felt were a concern. Sometimes peer pressure is a good thing!

Staff Memos

This is a useful tool that gives you a forum to share information, ideas, announcements, reminders, ask for input, and so on. It is kind of a written version of what staff meetings used to be.

This is the only place I would address problems with the entire group. Use the *complaining sandwich*, where you put something good on either side of the bad, and always let the good weigh as heavy as the bad.

Staff Meetings

- Use as a training tool or morale booster.
- Avoid complaining to the entire group.
- Address the few in private who need the lecture.
- Don't allow staff meetings to become morale busters!

Have a plan for the meeting, and allow the staff to help with the plan. This is not a time for you or the staff to air their complaints.

Allow staff to....

- Plan their meetings.
- Set the agenda.
- Plan the icebreaker.
- Do the training.
- Provide a team building exercise.
- Plan the refreshments or meal.

Chapter 7: Positive Supervision

Do you complain more than you praise? Let me remind you yet again that *whatever you focus on most is what you will get more of!*

I walked into a classroom one day and Laura, a staff member said, "What did we do now?" That was a wake up call for me. I took the opportunity to have a conversation with her. She was an awesome staff member and I valued her perspectives and perceptions. Once in a while, staff members will give you these little morsels of truth. Yes, it is *their* definition of the truth, which is based on *their* perception. When a staff member says something like that, we can either listen and find the learning morsel or become offended and walk away ticked off. Walking away in a huff just confirms the staff member's perception. Now, I get it that if we are hit with a morsel on the wrong day we may need to discuss it at a later time, in which case it is completely acceptable to say, "I would like to get your perspective on that. Can we talk about it tomorrow?" The worst way to handle the situation would be to get so upset that you would challenge the employee and have an altercation and/or reprimand the staff member right then and there. This trains your staff to never "speak the truth," for no one wants or deserves a dressing-down in public.

When I was working on my master's degree, I took a class from an energetic, spitfire professor. I knew Dr. Becky Bailey was going places, and she has written *the* book on classroom management. One of the gold nuggets I took away from her course was something you've already seen several times in this book: "Whatever you focus on most is what you will get more of!" That was not only a great lesson for the classroom but it also became a great life lesson. I know it seems self-explanatory, but I feel I need to expand on it with a couple of examples.

Classroom example: If Bob is a busy kid and you verbally reprimand him repeatedly, then the other children in the class will begin to tell whatever Bobby is doing that you should be reprimanding. Basically, you focus on the negative and now the other children will focus on the negative as well.

Life example: We all know or have had the employee that complains all the time. It is just one bad thing after another, and they'll share with anyone who will listen. Initially, we listen and may try to help, but after a while we realize it is never-ending and we aren't going to go along with that constant negative ride. I believe the complainer complains constantly because they are focusing on the negative constantly, and so that's all they see.

Who's the BOSS?

Holly Elissa Bruno says, "If the director isn't direct, who's in charge?" I wrote earlier about the typical non-aggressive personality of many directors. I believe that in order to be a great administrators, we must address issues or situations head-on.

Do not empower a challenging employee by ignoring their behavior!

Their power can be real or perceived. Silence is acceptance, so if your staff see you ignore the behavior, then that tells them you are okay with it. Either way threatens your authority and respect level.

Reprimanding the Individual

- Avoid "punishing" the whole group.
- Confront the individual.
- Staff morale will be damaged when entire group is disciplined.
- An Individual Problem requires and Individual Solution.
- Praise in Public.
- Confront or reprimand in Private.

When criticizing

- I will plan the conversation as to not come across angry.
- I will ensure not to project frustration or stress on staff who will take it.
- I will communicate one-on-one, in private.
- Criticism will be necessary, short, targeted, specific, direct, and objective.
- Criticism will be about the work and not the person.
- Criticism will end positively.
- Criticism will not be shared with others.
- Criticism will not change the way a staff member is treated.

Performance Appraisals

- Require staff to evaluate themselves.
- Administration evaluate the staff.
- Appraisals should be reflective.
- Employee should learn no new negative information (no surprises).
- Give raises that are earned. Raises should correlate to performance, education, etc.

Your Prize Employees

Treat them to a quick snack or cup of coffee at a local restaurant or in your office when evaluating their job performances and just chat!

I had employees who were excellent, and doing the performance appraisal became just a formality. So instead of going through the motions do something different. Leave the center and take them to get a drink and sit and chat for 15 minutes. This will be memorable for them and you.

Because I understand how childcare works, I know you cannot always leave the center If that is the case, then ask the Prize Staff what kind of drink they like and you just sit in your office and chat.

Chapter 8: Respecting Your Staff

This is a chapter that many would say is simply a given, and that I should not have to address it at all. Almost all administrators I have met who work in early childhood have been fundamentally good people. The issue I see is that when the administrator is under stress for long periods of time, they have a tendency to react to the staff in a shorter, more abrupt, and faster manner. Thus, the staff interprets this as the administrator being "bitchy." I don't use that word easily. I have tried to find another word that would have the same resonance and have not found one. I do not mean it in the historical or literal meaning, and it has nothing to do with male or female. I know I have been called a bitch many times over the years. This title is also given when staff members don't get their way when they ask for anything from a day off to supplies for their classrooms. The key to remember is who you are talking to; do not displace your frustration for others onto the staff members that happen to be in front of you. I am not a saint by any means, and I have had to apologize many times over the years for my handling of situations. Often it is not the message that gives us a bad rap – it is the *delivery*, by which I mean *how* we say it.

The Golden Rule

- Treat all staff w/ respect.
- Do not show favorites.
- All staff deserve respect regardless of education, age, experience, income, etc.

Often it is not that administrators have favorite employees, but it is the *appearance* or *perception* that they have favorites. One way to avoid this is to not make someone your go-to person. I have seen directors use staff as their "gofers," as in, "Go tell her this," "Go ask for that," and so on. Your gofer begins to be seen by other staff as the favorite, along with the concern that this staff member may also begin to develop an air of perceived authority. Now, if you have a staff member who is helping you in the office, or is your #2 or #3 employee in charge that is fine, just make sure everyone understands they are fulfilling that specific, assigned role at your request. Announce it clearly so there are no misperceptions!

Avoid socializing with the same one or two staff members when not working, going to lunch with a staff member on a regular basis, and anything else that can only lead to the speculation that they are your favorite. This is often an issue when an administrator has been promoted from within. Even if you treat your "friends" on staff equally, it still gives the perception of favoritism.

Always remember that there is a direct correlation between the respect and treatment you show your staff and the quality of your program!

Trickledown Quality

Owner

Area/Regional

Director

Staff (and their treatment of the children)

The better you treat your staff, the better they will treat the children!

When Parents Complain

Remember to listen to both sides!

- Don't assume the "parent is always right."
- Express to the staff that parent satisfaction and confidence is part of their job responsibility.
- Remember, people are our most important assets!

In theory, of course, you should always stand up for what is right. In practice, what is right is sometimes not totally clear. If we are truly objective, we can sometimes see some truth in both sides. What we must keep in mind is that *perception* is often different from *reality*.

Even if the staff did nothing wrong, the perception of the parent has to be considered. Keep the following in mind:

When enrollment is high: We gather information and decide who is right and deal with it, whether it means reprimanding a staff member or telling a parent they are wrong. Even if it means inevitably losing one of them.

When enrollment is low: Yes, in the real world, if our enrollment is low we are more willing to try and placate even a difficult parent for enrollment's sake. We must realize this is often at the expense of the morale of a staff member. Is there anything worse than doing your job and feeling unsupported or thrown under the bus by your boss? If you genuinely feel the best situation is for the employee to take more blame than they are responsible for, then the key is to be open and honest with the employee and say, "I need to handle it this way because we cannot afford to lose a child."

When dealing with challenging parents, we must be careful because sometimes it is easier to reprimand the staff member or placate the parent by telling them they are right and you agree. We must decide how to handle these situations because sometimes easy, short-term fixes can cause long-term problems.

Where DOES all the money go?

- Is your biggest priority the bottom line? Quality Childcare? Supporting your staff? Growing your customers?
- Find a balance!
- Be honest! Don't sugar-coat as to why a raise is not given.
- Don't flash luxuries in tough times.

You can "always do what's best for the children" and put yourself right out of business! It is a known fact that we must have a healthy balance in order to be a viable organization. I believe healthy organizations produce healthy children. If you or your staff are continually worried where your next paycheck will come from, that dysfunction seeps into the culture of the organization and most of your staff end up in the mindset of "looking something else." When that happens, they are never really totally engaged in the program.

I am a proponent of having a discussion and training with your staff on "where the tuition goes." Of course they don't need all the finest details, but the *reality* is probably much different than the *perception*. It also does not work to run around garnering sympathy because you aren't getting paid or you do not know how you are going to pay the bills. You become the director who cried wolf or you become white noise. Neither one is very effective long term.

It also works the opposite way. If you tell your staff you cannot afford raises this year and then drive up in a new Lexus, they can smell something fishy. I am sorry but the line, "My spouse is the one who makes the money" does not work after a while. I completely understand that the luxuries you own may have absolutely nothing to do with the success or profitability of your childcare program, but *perception* is *reality*. If you have it, do not flaunt it. Buy a less expensive car to drive to work and leave your big diamonds at home. Let me put it to you this way and then I'll leave it alone: If a client was coming into a welfare agency driving a new $50,000 car and wearing large diamonds, do they give the perception that they need assistance? The answer is clearly no.

The point to remember is to be honest with your staff. If you don't have it in the budget to do raises this year then say that, but don't say you cannot afford it if that is not the case. All of this can also be put into context with your parents and tuition.

Empower Staff

Participatory Management is the practice of empowering employees to participate in organizational decision-making. I especially love to use it in problem-solving. Allow staff to provide ideas and solutions. You'll be pleasantly surprised with the results. Remember, none of us are as smart as all of us!

Avoid the Us-Against-Them Mentality!

Who doesn't like to have choices? I know I prefer to be given a choice or asked for my input. It is a big turnoff and nearly offensive when I am told what to do. So when dealing with your employees, keep that in mind. If there is a way to solve a problem, make something better by asking the employees for input. When I have done this, my experience has been that I end up with viewpoints and ideas I had not thought of, and I end up with a better outcome, especially now because some employees have ownership of the decision.

Research shows that businesses where the employees opinions are higher have better…

- Productivity
- Profit
- Retention
- Customer satisfaction

Create an Atmosphere…

- That is open to change.
- Who tells you the truth?

As people in roles of authority, we earn credibility by being consistent and not wavering. We stand our ground. If you think about it, we can all think of a leader who became so entrenched in their way of doing things that the people around them would say, "They don't listen." So what I have learned is to listen to your staff! Have your ear to the rail. I've said it many times, and I'll say it again: Perception is reality! Once you have been a leader for a while, it is hard to relate to "what it was like" before. We see things from our perspective and we must have people around us who feel safe enough to tell us the truth and not just what we want to hear.

Cronyism is when a group of individuals work together and keep telling each other they are right and even when you are wrong you believe you're right because the people around you are agreeing with you. This can be frightening. It is hard to hear the truth sometimes, but it is necessary on a path to success. Have you ever had that boss who everyone was afraid of telling them the truth?

Input

- Get input from staff when interviewing new employees
- This allows staff to feel as if they had a part of the selection process
- Builds loyalty & dedication
- Review classroom assignments of children
- Give input on staff assignments
- Ask staff to evaluate administration annually

Committees

- Staff Activities
- Goals & Standards
- Accreditation
- Staff member on the Parent Committee

Developing committees is one of the most effective way to build loyalty, for staff to develop ownership, which in turn fosters buy-in. Of course, you can guide the committees' work, but this is one of those situations where if you let them work on their own, you will get better information and ideas then you would have by yourself.

If you are multi-site, try pulling a representative or two from each site to form an advisory committee. The buy-in you get from this is priceless. Staff appreciate having input, which makes them not feel as if things are thrust onto them with no choice. If you're too busy to attend a luncheon or meeting, send a staff member to represent the center. They'll appreciate playing an important role.

Chapter 9: Professionalism

Recognize

Diplomas & Certificates

Display awards in hallways, outside classroom doors, or in the center's foyer for maximum exposure. How impressive when doing a tour for a parent to see that the teacher was named teacher of the year! Announce awards when there is group activity such as a holiday party or children's program where friends, family, and peers are there to honor and congratulate

Acknowledge staff members' accomplishments, such as...

- Certifications
- Trainings
- Other accomplishments

And always say, "Thank you!"

Professional Needs

- Staff library filled with professional and personal development resources.
- Place in the staff lounge subscriptions to local newspapers, magazines, and newsletter, both educational and entertainment-based.

Be an example in handling staff and parents!

Encourage the use of…

- Note Cards
- Thank-you cards
- Business Cards for Teachers/Assistants

Practice Professionalism

Encourage the philosophy of the "Academic Year." The academic year is a philosophy I have been pushing for years. We have our Pre-K graduation in August just a week or two before school starts. This helps maintain our enrollment so we do not experience the typical drop that many centers have during the summer months.

Along with holding our graduation in August, we also do the majority of our move-ups around this time. We do not name our classrooms by age (for example the one-year-old class or three-year-old class). The reason we do this is because in the past we would have parents who wanted their child moved up to the next room on their birthday. They would often feel that if their child turns three and are still in the two-year-old room they would be missing out and would somehow fall behind in development.

We also try to focus as much as possible on making changes in staff during this time. Many times I have had staff wait to leave and give notice when they know it is time for children to move to their new rooms. There is rarely ever a good time for staff to leave, but it is much better that they leave *before* the children move up so the parents and the children do not have to experience the turnover.

Have Staff Refrain from Buying Supplies with Their Own Money

Budget the necessary funds to buy the supplies that are needed. The early childhood field is typically not a high-paying field, so staff members should not be expected to spend their own money buying supplies for their classrooms. I actually go further than just discouraging; I do not allow it at all. The other reason I do not allow staff to spend their own money is because they start feeling as if you "owe" them. In the long run this perpetuates a dysfunctional relationship and will ultimately frustrate your employees.

Keep the Facility and Equipment in Good Working Order

Maintenance is a challenge in almost any early childhood center. If you do not make an effort to stay on top of the maintenance, it will spiral out of control because the staff will assume you do not care and they will not care, which in turn worsens the problem. It is also very frustrating for a staff member to be hindered in doing their job due to broken or worn out equipment.

Chapter 10: Meeting Your Staff's Space Needs

Create a Personal, Comfortable Place for Staff
The Staff Lounge

Make the lounge feel homey, with comfortable adult furniture, relaxing light sources, etc. I do not enjoy lounges that look or feel like a doctor's office, classroom, or meeting room. A specified area allows staff to have a place where they can get away and/or connect with other staff.

- Provide a refrigerator (with ice maker), a microwave, and telephone.

- Provide condiments, TV trays, a table with a tablecloth, and a snack/drink machine.

- Have a Help Yourself Sharing Spot or Community Basket.

In the staff area, seasonally (or during stressful times) you should add some fresh flowers. Also designate a staff-only restroom if possible. If in your programs, like some of mine, you don't have a staff lounge, then set aside an area in the hall or afterschool room that the staff can use.

Staff Necessities

- A place to store their belongings.

- Furnish aspirin, ibuprofen, sinus medicine, Imodium, bandages, safety pins, etc.

There are two reasons I began offering over-the-counter medicine to my staff. Well, there's a whole story about the lady that had to leave to get a "feminine personal product" and never returned. Maybe she is still looking, but if she got lost she has been lost for a solid 10 years. I hope she realizes she is not on the clock. That would be some serious overtime! Anyway, I offer products to keep the staff at work. They would come up and say, "I have a headache," and then I could say, "Here's an aspirin." It just grew from there, and no, it does not bankrupt me to offer these products, nor has it ever been abused, but it has kept some staff at work that probably wanted to go home. That is almost always a good thing. And to clarify, I do not provide "feminine personal products."

Staff convenience

- Keep postage stamps on hand for employees to purchase.
- Allow the staff to leave their mail for postman to pick-up.

Encourage Your Staff to EAT with the Children

Encouraging the staff to eat lunch with the children accomplishes a couple things:

- It creates a positive atmosphere for the children and staff.
- It saves MONEY for the staff.
- It is encouraged by Accreditation and environment rating scales.

But the most important thing it does is this: It gives the staff the thought, "If I left I would have to buy myself lunch each day!"

Chapter 11: Get Parents Involved

Praise Tree

- Draw, paint, or build a tree with cut-out apples to act as "notes."
- Invite parents to give positive comments about staff members who go above and beyond the normal call of duty.
- Attach apples to the tree for all to view.

Build loyalty with your staff and your customers. Here are a few examples of ways to get your customers to show appreciation. I always learn great information when we do this activity. There are many examples of charts, trees, and murals, and you can check out Pinterest for tons of ideas. I recommend and I would often do this during the week of teacher appreciation, but it can be done around almost any time of year. Allow customers to continue adding and leave it up for a few weeks or a month.

Teacher Appreciation Week

I typically have always been a proponent of letting this week be about the parents showing their appreciation for the teachers rather than it being done by the center.

Create a form for parents to fill out, asking for their assistance and input for Teacher Appreciation Week activities. We always have a staff committee to help plan the activities for the week. Who better to tell us what they want than the staff themselves?

How to celebrate Teacher Appreciation Week started out very basic with signs announcing "Teacher Appreciation Week." Over the years it grew to include many more planned activities that the parents seemed to enjoy.

Now, typically the committee comes up with five activities, one to be assigned for each day of the work week. For some of the activities, we post a large poster for the parents to sign up on. This is very similar to the teacher sign-up form for covered dish lunches mentioned earlier.

We also have the staff to complete a "My Favorite" form to share with the parents. It has evolved and changed over the years to include the following:

- Favorite place to shop
- Favorite fast food restaurant
- Favorite color
- Favorite snack food
- Favorite drink
- And so on

Teacher Appreciation Week: Beach Theme

Example of the Week's Themes

Monday: Write a thank-you note to your child's teacher; we will also have a station set up in the lobby for you to complete it there if you like.

Tuesday: Buy your child's teacher lunch. For this we list the staff on a poster board in the lobby and the parents sign up to buy their child's teacher lunch. Yes, we always have multiple parents who want to buy the lunch, and yes, we always have a couple no one signs up to buy for. The center buys their lunch, but how informative is that? It is priceless!

Wednesday: Spa day! Surprise your child's teacher with any kind of spa supplies like lotions, sponges, bubble bath, etc.

Thursday: Gift Certificate Day.

Friday: Surprise your teacher day!

Typically on Friday, the center will have lunch catered for the staff. We have done anything from full catering, to box lunches, all way to having a food truck on site.

A Few Benefits to These Activities

- Spurs the staff to really kick up their performance.
- Gives the staff a well-deserved feeling of appreciation.
- As an administrator you get a first-hand opportunity to see who the parents really go all out for.
- It typically creates an atmosphere where parents get involved and become familiar with other parents at the center.
- As a result, friendships, center loyalty, and increased parental involvement will be the outcome.

Write Your Teacher a Note!

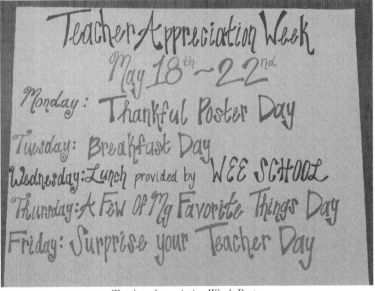

Teacher Appreciation Week Poster

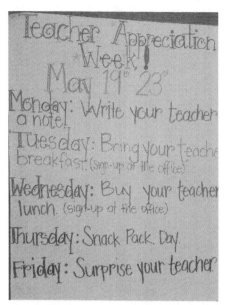

Another Teacher Appreciation Week Poster

Teacher Appreciation Notes - Butterflies

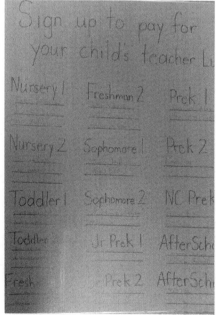

Parent Sign-Up to Buy Teachers' Lunches

Stories from Parents

- Develop appreciation letters to be filled out by parents
- Get feedback from parents on how a teacher has had a positive impact in their child's life
- Share compliments, praises, extra efforts received w/ staff to encourage continual growth & loyalty

Send a form home with parents asking them to share great stories. Set up a station in the lobby or hall with blank forms and pens so parents can take time to complete a form at pick-up, drop-off, or take it home. Have the parents or you post them in the lobby or on the classroom doors. When the activity is over, put some in the staff lounge and even convert a couple into testimonials for your program. You can also post some of them to social media outlets. Run a contest with your parents by asking them to post why they love their child's preschool and/or preschool teacher. The parent with the most likes and or shares wins the contest. This is a standalone activity or can be done in conjunction with Spirit Week or Teacher Appreciation Week.

Spirit Week

- Involve staff, parents, and children in various events to raise their morale and have fun.
- Staff activities and parent committees can handle planning.
- If staff help in planning, they have the buy-in factor.

Similar to Teacher Appreciation Week, we get the staff committee together to plan the activities for the week. This really spurs so much enthusiasm with the children, parents, and staff.

Each day we assign a theme and put up posters in the center in the weeks leading up to the week. Because I want 100% participation from the staff, we track who participates and we reward the ones who participate every day. We also have to keep in mind that staff have different personalities and comfort levels. For some, hat day is challenging, for Marcia, my longtime Assistant Director, she hated wearing hats. Then you have others who will walk around all day in pajamas with green hair.

Some Examples of the Themes

- Hat day
- Wear your favorite team colors day
- Wacky hair day
- Pajama day
- Storybook character day
- When I grow up day (occupation day)
- Wear your favorite color day
- Inside-out day
- Tacky day (Marcia struggled with this day also)
- Red, White and Blue day

Chapter 12: Benefits

You have to treat your employees well in order to retain them. One of the ways you can do that is to make sure they're getting a great array of benefits.

Supplemental Insurances

- Life
- Dental
- Vision

Depending on the number of employees, you may or may not have group health insurance. Due to the complexities I will not be attempting any kind of discussion of those details here.

I have spoken to directors who are of the mindset that if they do not offer health insurance, then they cannot offer any other insurance. That is wrong. Many small companies who do not offer group health insurance have decided to offer the best supplemental plans they can afford. Take note: Supplemental plans are quite inexpensive, but very valuable to employees.

Disability, Life, Dental, and Vision can all be arranged so that the employee pays 100%, therefore costing the company zero, or the company can decide to pay any percentage it can handle within its budget.

Life Insurance:

A couple years ago I had an employee die while working. Oh, and a grandparent was dropping off to her classroom when the employee collapsed. The grandparent still dropped off the child and just left. The things people do sometimes amaze me! Anyway, the employee was low-income and thank goodness for our life insurance, because that is what the family used to pay for her funeral.

After that I added life insurance for all employees as an added benefit. A $15,000 plan costs us around $20 a month, so it really doesn't have a major financial impact.

Disability Insurance:

Disability is very valuable in events such as an illness or pregnancy. When an employee becomes ill and cannot work, this insurance often keeps them out of foreclosure, and keeps cars from being repossessed.

We must keep in mind that many employees that work in early childhood are on the lower end of the income scale. They are often one paycheck away from a crisis, so anything within reason we can do to keep that from happening is wonderful for building employee loyalty.

Bonuses

- Monetary bonuses are great if at all possible.
- A bonus is a great sign of appreciation.
- The amount isn't so significant, but the act is invaluable.
- There are many ways of handling this, such as based on seniority, performance, attendance, etc.
- Budget for bonuses just like your mortgage!

Christmas Savings Plan

This optional program allows the staff to have a specific ongoing amount deducted from their paychecks so they'll have nice pot of money available for the holiday season by saving throughout the year. Make the check available well before the actual holiday on a specified date for planning purposes. It costs nothing to your center except the tiny price of printing the checks!

Chapter 13: Hiring, Orienting, and Training Right

My mantra when hiring is this: Take more time to make sure they are the right fit! Employers often confuse the areas *orientation* and *training*. A specific plan should be worked out for both. Orientation is like a "Welcome, here's the rules of the road," while training is more job specific skills needed to get the assigned work done.

Select and Interview Right

Screen the Applications

I recommend that whoever accepts the application (if it is hand-delivered), ask a question or two right then of the candidate. First impressions are priceless. Have the administrator who accepts applications make a note about their first impression. Have as many points of contact as possible before hiring. Do applicants have the correct credentials for the job? Make sure you ask them to bring verification of this for the interview, such as transcripts, licenses, and so on.

What have their job stays been like in terms of length? If you average their job stays, that is about how long they are going to stay with you. I love it when someone has 5 years of experience but at 6 different centers. Of course there are always exceptions, but job hoppers, although they generally interview well, will continue to be job hoppers. We often hire them out of desperation or optimism that they will like our center better than the others and stay.

Do an initial phone interview in order to go through some key points just to confirm what they put down is accurate. Ask specifically about breaks/gaps in employment. What did you do from _____ to ___?

Call their employment references. Make sure if it is their current employer that you have permission to call. Don't always ask for who they listed. Ask for the director. Sometimes employees will list coworkers instead of supervisors. Make sure you talk to who is/was in charge. If they are not available, then talk to whoever will talk to you. You would be surprised what the cook can tell you...

Schedule an Interview

Listen more than you talk. Give them a good up-to-date job description. Have them do an interactive observation in the classroom where they will be working and with the coworker they will be with if possible. After the observation, ask for input for your current staff. This gives them some buy-in because they feel as if they are a part of the selection process, which boosts their loyalty and dedication.

Schedule a second interview with another administrator if possible. If not, then you talk to them again. When you call to schedule, ask them what questions they might have about the job and/or the center. Then give them an assignment for the next interview. Complete an activity plan, bring their favorite book and watch them read to the children, etc. Ask them about something in the job description you gave them during the first interview.

A great question my friend Lara asks is this: "During the next 12 months, what do you have scheduled for which you will need time off?"

If you are having a hard time deciding between candidates do an old fashion pros/cons list to compare them.

Orient Right and Train Right

Orientation should happen as quickly as possible, and in small bite-sized pieces if possible. Employees are not going to remember all the information, so it is really more about going over it so they know where to find the information in your thorough Operations Manual or Employee Handbook.

Training should be conducted by your best employee. It does not matter if a toddler teacher trains a Pre-K teacher. If a weak teacher trains a new employee you will more than likely get weak training and potentially a new weak employee.

Mentors

A mentor can…

- Provide help and support for new or troubled employees.
- Revive employees, thereby reducing "burnout."
- Become a valuable resource.
- Give and receive new and exciting ideas.

When I use the word MENTORS, many directors groan, moan, and roll their eyes because many mentor programs are time-consuming and can be difficult to manage. That's why so many mentoring programs are not successful and get pushed down on the list of priorities of busy directors. But a mentoring program can be very simple. The ones I establish go like this: Match up a mentor and a mentee, introduce them to each other, and have them come up with a schedule of when they will interact with each other. Provide the mentor with money to take their mentee out to lunch every few weeks. Then you can reward your mentor when the new employee has stuck around for specific intervals, such as 30 days, 90 days, and one year.

Chapter 14: Professional Growth

How much time do you spend:

- Hiring...getting them in.
- Retention...keeping them in.
- Terminating...getting them out.

If you have been making doughnuts for five years, you are clearly a doughnut-maker. The early childhood field is interesting because so many go into it for a "meantime job" until something better comes along. If you are a director, when was the last time you read a professional development book? We need to stay on top of the best techniques and new ideas.

How much time do you spend on hiring (interviewing, training, TB's, physicals, orientation, criminal record checks, etc.)? It's important to realize that the worse your turnover rate, then the more time you spend on all these items.

Retention is all about appreciating, rewarding, acknowledging, interacting, building relationships, and empowering your employees. In a 40-50 hour work-week, how much time do you spend on retention? Most of us spend very little time here.

Also realize that supervising weak employees is where we spend the majority of our time!

Then there's all the time we spend on terminating, which might first include a re-training attempt, then documenting, conferencing, action plans, and letting them go if better results are not obtained. Of course we know there is a better use of all that time spent terminating. Wouldn't it be better to spend all that time on retention instead?

Do you have a retention plan? You should keep retention planning and activities going most all the time!

Mission Statement

Encourage the staff committee to update or create a motto/mission statement for their center.

Input

- Review classroom assignments of children.
- Give input on staff assignments.
- Ask staff to evaluate administration annually.
- Engage in Participatory Management.

Need a Quick Morale Boost? Unite Behind a Goal!

Find a common cause, such as licensing, accreditation, fundraising, an unpopular legislative item, or something else. Uniting behind some kind of goal brings individuals together to fight a larger battle.

Chapter 15: Conclusion

Be an Optimist

Staff look toward their directors for guidance and as an appropriate behavioral model. Strive for "a positive, upbeat attitude toward the world that sets you up for success…It enables you to overcome life's difficulties – to bounce back and thrive" (from *Learn to be an Optimist*, by Lucy MacDonald, 2004).

Always remember that your staff will never be more positive, excited, enthusiastic, committed, or optimistic than their director. As the director, you are the leader!

Martin Seligman, the father of learned optimism, says the following: "An optimist takes credit for good events [internal], believes that the positive effects will last [permanent] and that other aspects of his or her life will be affected [pervasive]. However, for bad events an optimist blames outside circumstances [external], maintains that the effect will not last [temporary] and that they are limited to this particular situation [specific]" (from *Learn to be an Optimist*, by Lucy MacDonald, 2004).

Self-Fulfilling Prophecies

"Our expectations first govern our intentions, which regulate our behavior, which affects the behavior of the other people involved" (from *Learn to be an Optimist*, by Lucy MacDonald, 2004). Obviously, this can be for better or for worse.

"If you think you can or if you think you can't, you're right."
~ Henry Ford ~

"Watch your thoughts, for they become words. Watch your words, for they become actions. Watch your actions, for they become habits. Watch your habits, for they become your character. And watch your character, for it becomes your destiny! What we think we become." ~ Margaret Thatcher.

What will you commit to change?

What will you do differently?

What are the obstacles?

I'm so glad you've read this book, but often we come to the end of something like this and we take our knowledge and notes back to the office and then the work hits us like a ton of bricks and we do nothing, I want you to commit right now that you're going to change something!

Obstacles

We will never have the perfect staff, money, benefits, support, equipment, or building we need. We can't say that we'll change or that we'll try when things turn around or get better. The reality is that you have to make the best out of what you have. Most of us are in the same situation, so let's agree to push through the barriers holding us back and do better!

BRIL: A New Leadership Model

By G. Sherman H. Morrison

I met Sherman Morrison recently and was pleased to discover his extensive knowledge on leadership and management. He was kind enough to share his own model of leadership, which I think can help put things in perspective for directors at a wide range of different centers and organizations. Enjoy!

Multiple Approaches to Leadership

What follows are brief summaries of a variety of approaches to leadership based primarily on Northouse (*Leadership: Theory and Practice*, 3rd Edition, 2004), with other sources cited as needed. My purpose in presenting thumbnail sketches of many approaches is to get the proverbial bird's eye view in order to see what themes emerge. Thus, I do so without attempting to group the approaches into any categories. I have found most such classification schemes to be of little or no value (a topic to which I will return later).

Trait Approach

The trait approach attempts to identify the personality attributes of effective leaders. Such traits typically include intelligence, self-confidence, determination, integrity, and sociability. One problem is that although mountains of research have been produced on leadership traits, there is still no agreed upon definitive set. Another problem is that traits are considered relatively fixed psychological features, which means leaders cannot really be developed or trained. Weighing in on the age-old nature/nurture debate, the trait approach falls squarely in the nature camp. One is either born to be a leader, or not.

Skills Approach

This approach, while recognizing that personality attributes do play a role, argues that there are also developable skills that leaders need to have. The skills model has three primary components: *Competencies* including problem-solving skills, knowledge, and social judgment skills (such as perspective taking or social intelligence, social perceptiveness, behavioral flexibility, and social performance); *individual attributes* including general cognitive ability, crystallized cognitive ability, motivation, and personality; and *leadership outcomes* including effective problem solving and performance. The leadership outcomes are the way to evaluate leadership effectiveness, which belies the approach's emphasis on problem-solving skills. *How* the components lead to leader effectiveness, however, is not explained by the theory. It should also be noted that this model was developed from military personnel and their performance in the armed services, calling into question the generalizability of the approach.

Style Approach

In the style approach, leadership behaviors generally fall into two primary categories: those focused on tasks (whatever it is the organization seeks to accomplish) and those focused on relationships (helping subordinates feel comfortable with themselves, each other, and the given situation). Some scholars have alternatively called these two categories *concern for results* and *concern for people*, *initiating structure* and *consideration*, or *production orientation* and *employee orientation*. The research in this approach has focused on describing how leaders behave, offering a way to asses one's own style, as well as to identify what style might be most effective, although the evidence on the lattermost point has been considered inconclusive. It does not have a strong situational component, and it is descriptive rather than prescriptive.

Situational Approach

This theory suggests that leadership needs to be tailored to the situation as defined by the changing needs of subordinates. The primary dimensions of leadership are composed of *directive* behaviors (to accomplish goals and achieve objectives) and *supportive* behaviors (helping subordinates feel comfortable with themselves, each other, and the given situation). Subordinates are assessed as to their level of *competence* and *commitment* for a given task, and the leader must then match the correct corresponding style to that situation. It is more prescriptive than the other approaches listed above.

Contingency Theory

This approach holds that the key to effective leadership is matching a leader's style to the correct setting. As with the style and situational approaches, leadership styles can be categorized as *task motivated* or *relationship motivated*. How it differs from the situational approach is that it greatly expands the concept of the situation beyond just the developmental level of subordinates to include *leader-member relations* (good or poor), *task structure* (high or low), and *position power* (strong or weak). Based on the diagnosis of the situation this theory will say which leadership style best fits that situation. The model suggests that when situational variables are extreme (either very smooth or very rough), task motivated leadership will be more effective than relationship motivated leadership. If the situational variables are moderate (things are neither totally out of control nor completely in control), relationship motivated leadership will be more effective than task motivated leadership. Interestingly enough, however, if there is a mismatch between the leadership style and the situation, the theory does not ask the leader to change or adapt their style to the situation (because leadership style is related to personality), rather the situation should be re-engineered to better fit the leader's style. In this approach, it becomes important for organizations to try to put the right leaders into the right situations.

Path-Goal Theory

This approach focuses on leadership to motivate subordinates to accomplish goals. It is once again a matching model, this time emphasizing the relationship between leadership style, subordinate characteristics, and the setting. It incorporates expectancy theory by acknowledging that employees will be motivated to do something if they think they are capable of doing it, if they can achieve a certain outcome, and if the payoff for doing it is worthwhile. The leader must help subordinates by filling in what is missing from the environment, and compensating for any deficiencies in their abilities. Although the leader needs to be familiar with subordinate characteristics, it is still heavily leader-centric, placing the onus on leaders to fill in everything employees need to achieve goals. Leadership behaviors described in this approach include both *directive* and *supportive* leadership (similar to previous theories), but adds in *participative* leadership in which the leader invites subordinates to participate in decision making, and *achievement-oriented* leadership that challenges subordinates to work the highest possible level.

Leader-Member Exchange Theory

The focus of this approach is to highlight the relationship that occurs between a leader and each follower. The prescriptive part of this approach indicates that leaders should strive to develop high-quality exchanges with each follower. These exchanges develop over time from stranger to acquaintance to mature partnership. The leader must look for ways to develop high-quality relationships of trust, respect, and obligation with each follower so that their motive changes from self-interest to the good of the organization. The model is weak, however, in explaining just how this is to be accomplished. The descriptive component of the model is very accurate in describing how leaders make more use of some followers (who become the "in-group") and less of others (who become the "out-group").

Transformational Leadership

Transformational leadership focuses on how visionary, charismatic leaders are able to understand the needs and motives of followers, connecting with them in a way that helps them to reach their fullest potential. In the process, both the leader and follower are transformed to new levels of motivation and morality. More specifically, transformational leaders are strong role models, highly moral/ethical, inspire others to rise above self-interest, encourage creativity and innovation, are highly attentive to followers' needs, offer a clear vision, create trust, recognize the need for and precipitate change, and finally institutionalize that change. As a leadership theory, it is very close to being a change model, clearly viewing leadership and change as inextricably bound together. On the nature/nurture debate, transformational leadership swings the pendulum back towards the nature end of the spectrum in that it depends to some degree on the charisma of the leader. It is a leader-centric approach, for in spite of part of the model being about the needs of followers, it is still centered on the leader doing things to move the followers. Transformational leadership is often contrasted with *transactional* leadership, which rather than focusing on the needs of subordinates or their personal development instead trades rewards and/or punishments for desired behaviors. In even greater contrast is *laissez-faire* leadership, which is essentially the absence of any leadership.

Team Leadership

The team approach has become very popular, begging the question of the role of team leadership to effective teams. Two critical components of team leadership are *team performance* (task focus) and *team development* (relationship focus). Team leadership must constantly focus on both to make an effective team. The model recognizes the importance of paying attention to both the internal environment (the task and relational needs of the team) and the external environment (to which the team must adapt), and the need to know when to react by changing or staying the course. Key to this approach is skill in continual diagnosing, and having a repertoire of interventions when action is needed. The eight characteristics of effective teams that leaders must achieve are 1) Clear, elevating goal; 2) Results-driven structure; 3) Competent members; 4) Unified commitment; 5) Collaborative climate; 6) Standards of excellence; 7) External support and recognition; 8) Principled leadership (willingness to confront inadequate performance; not being too easy; personal commitment to team goal; allow member autonomy).

Psychodynamic Approach

The emphasis in this approach is self-knowledge for leadership and followership. The point here is not to match behaviors and styles to particular situations or subordinate needs, but to achieve a high level of self-understanding, and thereby understand how one responds to others. The influence of psychotherapy is strong in this approach, which advocates understanding of one's family history, maturation or individuation, and any number of other psychological concepts. It is essentially and understanding of leadership through the concepts and language of psychology. By understanding the psychological dynamics at play, one can then learn to avoid or change unwanted patterns of behavior and reactions, as well as better understand the behaviors and motivations of others, especially their reactions to you. A basic problem with this approach is that most psychological theories and concepts were developed by studying people with serious difficulties, and are also very subjective based on the researcher's own biases (including culture and social class). The psychodynamic approach also largely ignores various organizational factors.

Adaptive Leadership

In this approach, Heifetz (*Leadership without easy answers*, 1994) draws a basic distinction between routine or *technical* challenges and *adaptive* challenges. The latter tend to be systemic problems with no easy answers, problems that challenge deeply held beliefs and values, and that involve a variety of legitimate but competing perspectives. Dealing with adaptive challenges requires leadership that does six specific things: 1) *Getting on the balcony* to get the big-picture view of what is happening, and to be able to move from the field of play to the balcony and back; 2) Identifying the adaptive challenge by looking closely at root causes of systemic problems; 3) *Regulating distress* by creating a "holding environment" in which adaptive work can safely take place, setting direction by framing the key questions, protecting by managing the rate of change, orienting by defining realities and key values, instilling conflict as a means to creativity, and shaping norms, all the while maintaining presence and poise, including the emotional capacity to tolerate uncertainty, frustration, and pain; 4) *Maintaining disciplined attention* to the adaptive challenge, involving everyone with their different experiences, assumptions, values, beliefs, and habits (which many people would rather avoid through scapegoating, denial, etc.) by asking the right questions, reframing the debates, and unbundling issues; 5) *Giving the work back to the people* in order to avoid the tendency of leadership to offer solutions which by rights should come from the people, empowered by the leader to participate in solving the problem; 6) *Protecting voices of leadership from below* by making sure all the stakeholders can participate, even those that seem difficult or that are often otherwise excluded.

Servant Leadership

This approach, summarized by Smith, Montagno and Kuzmenko (Transformational and servant leadership: Content and contextual comparisons. *Journal of Leadership & Organizational Studies*, 10(4), 80-91, 2004) is about placing as much emphasis on followers as can be achieved. A leader first is a servant, and only subsequently is perceived as a leader, typically by the urging of others and not themselves. The true servant leader's primary motivation is to serve, not to lead. Specific skills and characteristics of servant leaders include listening, empathy (recognizing, respecting, accepting, and understanding others), healing (both for oneself and others), awareness (general and self-awareness), persuasion (as opposed to simple positional authority), conceptualization (nurturing abilities and thinking big), foresight (learning from the past, accounting for present realities, and understanding future consequences of decisions), stewardship (holding something in trust for others), helping others develop (eventually to become servants themselves), and building community. Other themes important to this approach include paying particular attention to social justice, making sure the "have-nots" are included, removing inequalities, shifting authority to followers, and in general placing the needs of followers ahead of self interests.

Authentic Leadership

In this approach, the overriding emphasis is on knowing and being true to oneself. As one group of scholars put it, "Authentic leaders demonstrate a passion for their purpose, practice their values consistently, and lead with their hearts as well as their heads. They establish long-term, meaningful relationships and have the self-discipline to get results. They know who they are." (George, Sims, McLean, & Mayer, Discovering your authentic leadership, *Harvard Business Review*, 85(2), 129-138, 2007). It begins with understanding one's life story, putting hard work into self-development, and eschewing the need for public acclaim and financial reward in favor of strong intrinsic motivations. Gardner et al ("Can you see the real me?" A self-based model of authentic leader and follower development. *The Leadership Quarterly*, 16(3), 343-372, 2005) expanded the notion of authentic leadership to include followers who, by following the model provided by authentic leaders, develop into authentic followers and thereby experience heightened levels of trust, engagement, and well being. They also emphasized the relational aspect of authentic interactions between leaders and followers and the eventual achievement of "organizational climates that are more inclusive, caring, engaged, and more oriented towards developing strengths."

Relational Leadership Theory

This theory, as laid out by Uhl-Bien (Relational leadership theory: Exploring the social processes of leadership and organizing. *The Leadership Quarterly*, 17(6), 654-676, 2006) notes that while many approaches to leadership have placed an emphasis on the importance of relationships (leader-member exchange being the most prominent to do so), they have largely looked at relationships from a static, dyadic point of view, perhaps attempting to characterize their quality, but not going beyond that. By contrast, relational leadership theory, coming from a distinctively post-modern philosophical base, focuses on the *process* of relationships. It sees leadership and all organizational phenomena as emerging from within relationships and constructed by processes of relating. Leadership becomes the processes by which social order (including attitudes, values, and goals) is constructed and changed. This approach emphasizes the importance of communication in the relational process, as well as leadership being inseparable from the context in which it emerges.

Complexity Leadership Theory

This approach draws heavily upon complexity science and its implications for leadership. Complexity leadership theory (CLT) recognizes the following three broad forms of leadership:

> (1) leadership grounded in traditional, bureaucratic notions of hierarchy, alignment and control (i.e., administrative leadership), (2) leadership that structures and enables conditions such that CAS are able to optimally address creative problem solving, adaptability, and learning (referring to what we will call, enabling leadership); and (2) leadership as a generative dynamic that underlies emergent change activities (what we will call, adaptive leadership). (Uhl-Bien, Marion, & McKelvey, Complexity leadership theory: Shifting leadership from the industrial age to the knowledge era. *The Leadership Quarterly*, *18*(4), 298-318, 2007)

CLT highlights the importance of context to leadership, not as an antecedent, mediator, or moderator variable, but as the ambience from which leadership is spawned. Another key feature of CLT is the importance of maintaining flexibility rather than rigidity or control. Leadership must be seen as connective, distributed, dynamic and contextual. *Enabling* leadership becomes the bridge or balancing point between *administrative* leadership and *adaptive* leadership.

From the above presentation of brief sketches of a variety of approaches, I identify five emergent themes:

1. Nature and Nurture: Some approaches clearly think of leadership potential as something fixed at birth, while others recognize it as something that can be developed.

2. Many, if not most, approaches are very focused on the leader as an individual. A few of the theories attempt to give some more weight to followers.

3. A surprising number of the approaches have absolutely nothing to say about the context in which leadership takes place. Some provide a very rudimentary consideration of context, and others provide a robust view of context.

4. Some approaches are heavily descriptive, often of leaders rather than leadership, and offer little in the way of prescriptive ideas. Other approaches attempt to do both to some degree.

5. Some approaches focus on the tasks or work of the organization (production), while others recognize that relationships among the people of the organization are important, while still others recognize the importance of both, and some ignore the production/people question altogether.

Because these five themes are present throughout leadership theories, and involve so many fine shades of distinction, there can be no simple grouping of theories into categories that does justice to the inherent complexity of all five themes. Any such taxonomy is, in my opinion a fruitless endeavor.

When faced with such a variety of approaches, one might attempt to determine which is the best or right theory, but in doing so fall prey to a debilitating reductionism. This is not uncommon in the social sciences. George Cowan, when he was president of the Santa Fe Institute, described it well when he said "The usual way debates are conducted now in the social sciences is that each person takes a two-dimensional slice through the problem, and then argues that theirs is the most important slice. 'My slice is more important than your slice, because I can demonstrate that [in the case of the federal government's role in the economy] fiscal policy is much more important than monetary policy,' and so forth" (Waldrop, *Complexity: The Emerging Science at the Edge of Order and Chaos.* New York, Simon & Schuster 1992, p. 342). Each approach reviewed above can be considered just such a two-dimensional slice. Each contains both strengths and weaknesses, but when viewed in isolation each one represents only a portion of a much larger, complex picture. The opportunity that arises from this challenge of multiple approaches is a chance to honor the full richness of a complex field of study.

Toward a More Balanced Approach to Leadership

When I examine the different approaches to leadership closely, I inevitably find that something is missing or something is out of balance in each one. What I've done is take the important emergent themes from the different theories and combine them into something I call *Balanced Reflective Intelligent Leadership* (BRIL). Descriptively, it includes the following four spheres of intelligence: Self-Intelligence, Relational Intelligence, Contextual Intelligence, and Reflective Intelligence. Prescriptively, these then become arenas for development, practice, and training as follows: Self-Development, Relational Practice, Contextual Sensitivity, and Reflective Practice. These elements may be thought of as nested spheres that can be presented visually as concentric circles.

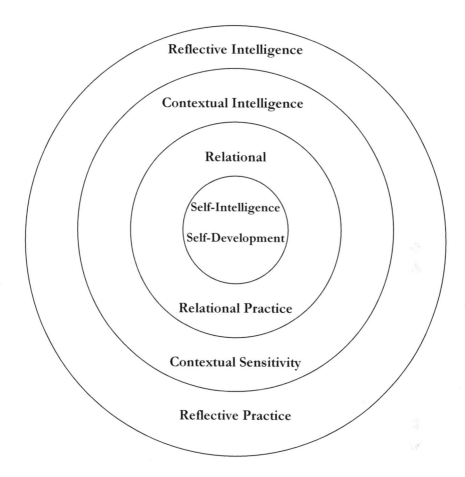

As seen above, *self-intelligence* is at the core of leadership. From this core, leadership expands into relating to others (relational intelligence), and then expands further to awareness and understanding of the context in which leadership takes place (contextual intelligence). Finally, reflective intelligence is the outermost sphere that encompasses, penetrates, and informs the other three.

Within each sphere of intelligence, there are contrasting elements that must be brought into balance. This balance, however, should not be thought of as some kind of static equilibrium, but a dynamic, ever-shifting harmony based on continual learning and the needs of the situation. What follows are details on each sphere of the BRIL approach.

Self-Intelligence and Self-Development for Leadership

Socrates is one of several ancient Greek sages to whom has been attributed the well-known exhortation to "Know thyself." Self-knowledge and self-awareness are important features to be incorporated into leadership practice. Clearly, leadership is more than a mere collection of fixed personality characteristics as suggested by the trait approach. Jackson and Parry (*A very short, fairly interesting and reasonably cheap book about studying leadership*, 2008) summarize the age-old nature/nurture debate this way: "Refreshingly, the conclusion seems to be that it is a 50-50 bet. Yes, heredity and pedigree determine some elements of leadership, but the experiences that we have at home and in life determine our leadership capabilities just as much."

Knowledge of one's traits can help leaders be more aware of their own limitations as well as their strengths. This sphere of intelligence draws mainly from the *trait approach, skills approach, psychodynamic approach*, and *authentic leadership*, all of which placed emphasis on self-knowledge. The challenge in this sphere is to achieve balance along the nature/nurture continuum, which can also be thought of as the traits/skills continuum.

On the practical side, any number of psychometric instruments may be taken to achieve a higher level of self-knowledge about one's traits, including the Myers-Briggs Type Indicator, the PACE Palette, the Kolb Learning Style Inventory (LSI), and 360° Feedback. More information about these learning tools is readily available on the Internet, and some can be purchased and taken online.

The self-knowledge that is gained, however, must be balanced by an examination of skills. Knowing where one stands on various skill sets is also a useful endeavor. For this aspect of increasing self-knowledge, specific instruments that might be explored include the Leadership Skills Inventory (LSI), Leadership Skills Profile (LSP), and the Emotional Competence Inventory (ECI). Once again, more information on these and other instruments can be readily obtained from the Internet.

Relational Intelligence and Practice for Leadership

Self-intelligence for leadership, although essential, must be complemented by an exploration of how leaders relate to their peers and subordinates. Most of the assessment instruments referenced above contain explicit information directed at how leaders relate to others, and should be applied in this realm of relational practice as well. The balance sought within this sphere of intelligence is focusing not only on the tasks of the organization, but also the relationships through which leadership occurs (a basic point brought out in the *style approach*). As Jackson and Parry put it: "If you strike the right balance between concern for people and concern for production, you will be the most effective leader." Another point of balance to be achieved in this sphere is exhibiting both directive and supporting behaviors (as laid out in the *situational approach*), providing the right mix of both depending on the needs of subordinates and the urgency of production.

Contextual Intelligence and Sensitivity for Leadership

Tony Mayo, in his Harvard Business Review blog, explains what he means by *contextual intelligence* this way:

> There is far too much focus on individual characteristics of leadership and far too little focus on the situational context.

By placing too much emphasis on the individual, we can easily fall prey to the cult of the CEO and believe that any individual who was successful in one setting would naturally be successful in a new setting. The list of once-successful CEOs who have failed in new business settings is long.

Leadership theories advanced greatly when they began to take into account the context of leadership, including both internal organizational culture and the myriad external market and other environmental forces applying pressure to leaders and organizations. Leaders must become adept at diagnosing organizations relative to their cultures and the larger environments in which they operate.

Reflective Intelligence and Practice for Leadership

Perhaps the most important sphere of all is reflective intelligence and practice. Without it, leadership cannot increase in effectiveness. Extending and deepening one's self-knowledge, and understanding how one is perceived by and relates to others, and being sensitive to the context in which leadership occurs, will all be an exercise in futility if it is not accompanied by a robust reflective practice. This must involve two different levels of reflection as described by Schön (*The reflective practitioner: How professionals think in action*, 1983). One is called *reflection-in-action*, otherwise known as "thinking on your feet," in which you reflect just enough in a situation that is unfolding to build an understanding that informs your actions, drawing upon both past experiences and current feelings. The other level of reflection is called *reflection-on-action*, which entails carving out a more substantial period of time in which to look back at situation and analyze it on a deeper level. Clearly, the two go hand-in-hand. The challenge, of course, is finding the time in busy schedules for reflection-on-action!

Annotated Bibliography

There are so many books out there to choose from that can help you be a better director, supervisor, manager, or leader. Below is listing of some of the best you can read. There's a lot here, and you certainly don't need to read them all, but choose the ones that feel like they might have been written just for you!

- Alberti, R.E. & Emmons, M.L., *Your Perfect Right: A Guide to Assertive Living (6th Ed.).* Impact Publishers, 1990. Any book on assertiveness that's sold more than 1.25 million copies is probably worth a look, and this one does not disappoint! It is chock full of detailed how-to steps and examples, along with lots of exercises to help you become more assertive. This is an essential skill as a director, manager, supervisor, or leader.

- Arapakis, M., *Softpower: How to Speak Up, Set Limits, and Say No Without Losing Your Lover, Your Job, or Your Friends.* Warner Books, 1990. This one is especially geared towards to women to make sure they can handle all the different challenges they face, whether in the workplace or at home or out in the community while maintaining self-respect and good relationships.

- Belenky, M. et al., *Women's Ways of Knowing: The Development of Self, Voice, and Mind.* Basic Books, 1986. Women have come a long ways in modern society, but it's still shocking how few make it into the upper echelons of corporate or government leadership. The book contains in-depth interviews with scores of women to reveal how so many still feel silenced today. The conclusion is clear: While women's ways of knowing are oftentimes different from men, they are vitally needed in the 21st century!

- Bell, C., *Managers as Mentors: Building Partnerships for Learning.* Bard Press, 1998. This is a fairly quick read but packs a powerful punch. Too many out there roll their eyes at the idea of mentoring programs, but I have found them to be incredibly effective at quickly getting new staff up to speed and performing well. A fictional mentoring relationship provides context throughout the book, as well as practical applications for its ideas. Once you've read this book, you'll realize just what you're missing out on by not having a robust mentoring program.

- Bellman, G., *Getting Things Done When You Are Not in Charge.* Berrett-Koehler, 1992. What do you do when you don't really have any formal authority but still need to get things done? It's not impossible, but it does take some specific strategies. This one is useful for directors because it gives you insight to the challenges your staff may face when they don't feel like they have the right level of authority to do thing.

- Bennis, W., *Managing People is Like Herding Cats.* Executive Excellence, 1997. Have ever tried to herd cats? It really doesn't work, at all. And managing people can often feel that way. This is one of those times where you have to distinguish between management and leadership. Yes, as a director you have plenty of management functions you have to fill, but you also have to be a leader if you want your people to stick around and do great work for you. One of your primary skills in this regard is to facilitate change in a way that is both effective and senstitive.

- Bennis, W. & Biederman, P., *Organizing Genius: The Secrets of Creative Collaboration.* Addison-Wesley, 1997. For your organization to be successful, you need everyone working together in a collaborative manner. In this book, the author looks at six highly successful examples for lessons that can be used by any organization.

- Block, P., *The Empowered Manager: Positive Political Skills at Work*. Jossey-Bass, 1987. Anything by Peter Block is worth reading, and you'll see I've listed several more of his books below. He's an incredibly clear and effective writer. In this book he focuses on the management side of the organizational equation, explaining everything you need to know to be an effective manager, and I love his focus on relationships and interactions between different people in the organization.

- Block, P., *Stewardship: Choosing Service Over Self-Interest*. Berrett-Koehler, 1993. I'm big on having a bigger purpose in one's work life than just punching the clock and collecting paychecks. Think about how transformative your center would be if all your staff thought about what they do every day as *service* rather than just as a job to be done. Well, there are things you can do to spread that attitude throughout your organization, and this book explains how to do it.

- Block, P., *Flawless Consulting: A Guide to Getting Your Expertise Used (2nd Ed.)*. Jossey-Bass/Pfeiffer, 2000. I'm including this one because once you've got a lot of experience under your belt as a center director or owner, it can make a lot of sense to expand your horizons by engaging in consulting projects to help others learn from your experience. I've been doing a lot of that lately, and I find it to be very invigorating and satisfying. With this book, you'll learn a lot about what it takes to get into it.

- Block, P., *The Only Answer to How is Yes: Acting on What Matters*. Berrett-Koehler, 2003. Okay, this is the last Peter Block book I'll put in here, but it's an important one. Too many people become paralyzed and fail to take needed action because they think they don't know how to do what needs to be done. Block's point here is that you probably know more than you think, and you can always still take some effective action.

- Bolman, L. & Deal T., *Leading with Soul: An Uncommon Journey of Spirit (3rd Edition)*. Jossey-Bass, 2011. This one has inspired thousands of leaders since it was first published back in 1995. In today's tumultuous times, how do love and power fit together? Find out in this very personal journey of one executive in his search for meaning.

- Bolton, R., *People Skills: How to Assert Yourself, Listen to Others, and Resolve Conflicts*. Simon & Schuster, 1986. This can easily become your go-to handbook to address all kinds of communication issues. The author reviews a dozen of the things that most often get in the way of good communication, and havoc they wreak on all your relationships. If what you need is a new approach to more effective and clear communication, don't pass on this timely and relevant book. It's especially good on communication in high-stress or intensely-charged emotional situations.

- Branden, N., *How to Raise Your Self-Esteem: The Proven Action-Oriented Approach to Greater Self-Respect and Self-Confidence*. Bantam Books, 1987. It's hard to run any kind of organization if you're lacking self-esteem, and most people feel that lack at some point or other in their lives. The message is clear: Low self-esteem results in passive inaction and failure, while higher self-esteem leads to proactive success. This book is written by a psychologies who helps you take concrete steps to improve how you see your own worth. And don't we all want to feel better about ourselves?

- Branden, N., *Self-Esteem at Work: How Confident People Make Powerful Companies*. Jossey-Bass, 1998. It's interesting to read the last book and this one together or right after each other. In this book the author takes his considerable knowledge about self-esteem and how to raise it and applies it in the workplace. You won't find anyone with a better understanding of self-esteem and the difference it can make to your career.

- Branham, L., *The 7 Hidden Reasons Employees Leave: How to Recognize the Subtle Signs and Act Before It's Too Late.* AMACOM, 2005. If you want to do a better job at tackling turnover, you've got to understand *why* people leave in the first place. This isn't always easy, as people will give you all kinds of reasons that aren't the *real* reason. It's usually not about the money or benefits (although it can be). It usually has more to do with a variety of negative aspects in the organization. Your task is to firmly eliminate those negatives for better retention.

- Buckingham, M. & Coffman, C., *First, Break All The Rules: What The Worlds Greatest Managers Do Differently.* Simon & Schuster UK Ltd, 2000. What is it that great managers do differently from others? That's the question Buckingham and Coffman answer in this important book. According to their research, it's really about selecting new hires based on talent rather than specific skills or experience. Just as important is setting clear expectations and playing to people's strengths in a way that motivates them for peak performance. They also pay attention to making sure the person is a great fit for the organization.

- Burley-Allen, M., *Managing Assertively: How to Improve Your People Skills (2nd Ed.)* Wiley, 1995. Everyone knows that managing a center in the 21st century is all about people skills, and this book will definitely turbo-boost your management knowledge in very helpful ways, including conflict resolution through much better communication skills, increased self-awareness, and all kinds of exercises to build your competencies.

- Clance, P., *The Impostor Phenomenon: Overcoming the Fear that Haunts Your Success.* Peachtree Publishers, 1985. I think nearly everyone knows what it's like when you feel like an imposter – it's that feeling that you don't really belong where you're at because you doubt your abilities or knowledge. It's hard to be successful if you don't even feel like you should be where you're at. This book helps you overcome that difficulty.

- Cohen, A. & Bradford, D., *Influence Without Authority.* Wiley, 1990. There are those who think leadership is all about influence, but what happens when you haven't been given any authority? Can you still exercise influence? The answer is not only YES, it's more like you MUST. Anytime you're faced with being held accountable for results without direct authority, this is the book you need to navigate those murky waters. It will show you how you can still get plenty of cooperation even when lacking authority.

- Crawley, J., *Constructive Conflict Management: Managing to Make a Difference.* Nicholas Brealey Publishing, 1995. Conflict in the workplace is inevitable. What matters is how you deal with it. The key is to try and get people to work *through* differences and still get the job done, while at the same time avoiding hurting each other in the process. For managers, you'll be able to see how the author works through all kinds of common conflicts encountered with great results. It's about understanding and self-awareness.

- Crowley, K. & Elster, K., *Working With You Is Killing Me: Freeing Yourself From Emotional Traps at Work.* Warner, 2006. These two women make a great combination – one is a psychologist and the other is a management expert. Together they reveal what you can do when your coworkers are simply driving you crazy. When your workplace relationships leave you feeling bewildered, drained, or at worst wanting to quit, this book shows you how to deal with it effectively.

- Dreher, D., *The Tao of Personal Leadership.* Harper Business, 1997. This is an important book that tries to swing the pendulum away from competition and towards cooperation. The emphasis here is on renewal, vision, harmony, and good communication, all inspired by the ancient wisdom of Taoist principles. This one works well for both managers and leaders.

- Deep, S. & Sussman, L., *What to Say to Get What You Want: Strong Words For 44 Challenging Types Of Bosses, Employees, Coworkers, And Customers.* Addison-Wesley, 1992. Sometimes it's hard to know what to say that will lead you to the outcomes you seek. That's why this is such a handy little book. Whether it's the perfectionist boss or annoying coworkers that siphon away valuable time, this book gives you the words you need to get the results you want.

- Deep, S. & Sussman, L., *Smart Moves for People in Charge: 130 Checklists to Help You be a Better Leader.* Perseus Books, 1995. When work gets complicated, it can be hard to remember all the little (and big) things that go into making you a great leader. The beauty of this book is that its content is presented in a valuable series of checklists that quickly remind you of all the important practices you need to be using to be a good leader.

- Deep, S. & Sussman, L., *Act on It! Solving 101 of The Toughest Management Challenges.* Perseus Books, 2000. As you can see, these books by Deep and Sussman are important, in part because they're so practical in how they break things down for you. In this one, the authors apply their pragmatic approach to the age-old task of problem-solving. Whether it's holding your people accountable or navigating the maze of human resources tasks such as hiring and firing, this book walks you through simple but very effective problem-solving techniques that will help you get superior results.

- DePree, M., *Leadership is an Art.* Dell Books, 1989. This is a book that gets widely read not just in business but in all kinds of fields because of its powerful insights. First published in 1989, it has sold more than 800,000 copies since then. His focus within leadership is on the need to build up good relationships, which is one of my own focal points as well in my work. He also covers the importance of how leaders define reality in an organization, create lasting systems of value, and initiate new ideas. Just like me, he also emphasizes how important it is to thank people.

- DePree, M., *Leadership Jazz: The Essential Elements of a Great Leader.* Doubleday/Currency, 1992. Another DePree book worth reading, this one is all about how to be in tune with the people you're leading or managing, and how sometimes you have to let them take the wheel and drive from time to time. When you learn to do that, you'll find you get a lot more out of your people than before.

- DePree, M., *Leading Without Power: Finding Hope in Serving Community.* Jossey-Bass, 1997. One more DePree book here, this time one that focuses on the service aspect of leadership, which I find is really essential. Rather than making leadership about the exercise of formal power, he makes the point here that it's more about the level and kind of freedom your people have in the organization. It's both refreshingly simple and profoundly difficult to achieve, but worth the effort.

- Douglas, E.F., *Straight Talk: Turning Communication Upside Down for Strategic Results at Work.* Davies-Black, 1998. No doubt your own experiences in the workplace have included all manner of thorny issues. This book is a great example of how to tackle those issues with better, more skillful communication.

- Driscoll, R., *The Stronger Sex: Understanding & Resolving the Eternal Power Struggles Between Men & Women.* Prima, 1998. Even in the 21st century it still feels like men are from Mars and women are from Venus. Why is it still so difficult to get men and women on the same page? This books reveals why, and how you can achieve a better understanding of those differences in order to work effectively with them.

- Ellinor, L & Gerard, G., *Dialogue: Rediscover the Transforming Power of Conversation.* John Wiley & Sons, 1998. Communication is such a key skill in modern times, and this book's emphasis is on the dialog aspect of communication. It helps you better converse and think with others in ways that foster partnerships and collaboration rather than allowing differences to get in the way. Even better, it helps you figure out how to dialog on what matters most. Concepts important in this approach include trust, a spirit of inquiry, and mutual respect.

- Fisher, R. & Sharp, A., *Getting It Done: How to Lead When You Are Not in Charge.* Harper Business, 1998. This book is all about how to work more effectively with people towards common goals, even when you're not the one who's in charge of everything.

- George, B., *Authentic Leadership: Rediscovering the Secrets to Creating Lasting Value.* Jossey-Bass, 2003. Being authentic in your organization is one of the most important things you can do as a leader. This book was written in the midst of all kinds of corporate scandals and includes many personal stories of the author in leading a major business as authentically as possible.

- Glaser, C. & Smalley B., *Swim with the Dolphins: How Women Can Succeed in Corporate America on Their Own Terms.* Warner Books, 1995. Women have a particularly tough time in the business world, but this book shows how many women succeed as managers without just giving in to the rules of the road in "man's world." The message is that women can succeed by leveraging their traditional traits of nurturing and caring for others.

- Goleman, D, & McKee, A., *Primal Leadership: Learning to Lead with Emotional Intelligence.* Harvard Business Books, 2004. You've no doubt heard of *emotional intelligence*. This is the book that really vaulted the concept into the popular mind. There's really no way to be an effective leader today without emotional intelligence. It includes such concepts as self-awareness, empathy, motivation, and collaboration.

- Griffin, J., *How to Say It at Work: Power Words, Phrases, and Communication Secrets for Getting Ahead (2nd edition)*. Prentice Hall, 2008. In this updated edition, the author includes a whole new chapter on digital communication, which is clearly an essential in the 21st century. One of the greatest parts of this book is how it teaches you to build an effective and persuasive argument for something, and how to disagree with others without being a jerk.

- Grothe, M. & Wylie, P., *Problem Bosses: Who They Are and How to Deal with Them*. Fawcett Crest, 1987. Whether you are or are not a boss, this one is definitely worth reading. There are way too many problem bosses out there, and you don't want to be one, so see if you recognize yourself in this book!

- Halpern, B.L. & Lunar, K., *Leadership Presence*. Gotham Books, 2003. This one is really interesting because it takes ideas from being on the theatrical stage and applies them to leadership. Having never really thought of the two together before, I was struck by how relevant the message and advice are in this book.

- Helgesen, S., *The Female Advantage: Women's Ways of Leadership*. Doubleday/Currency, 1990. No surprise here to find that men and women approach work in very different ways. But more specifically, women also lead organizations and evolve their structures very differently, and in ways that often tend to work better than the defaults of men. The organizations that women lead tend to be flatter, more creative, and more collaborative. She follows four successful women leaders and how they do what they do. It's an invaluable resource for anyone who wants to be a better leader.

- Helgesen, S., *The Web of Inclusion.* Doubleday/Currency, 1995. This other book by Helgesen is also important. It's about sweeping away the old structures that keep people in rigidly defined roles and instead makes everything more inclusive. This necessarily involves greater flexibility and interconnectedness, all of which is more achievable than ever before. She also goes into detail about five organizations that are actually doing it.

- Hill, L.A., *Becoming a Manager: How New Managers Master the Challenges of Leadership.* HBS Press, 2003. New managers have a tough row to hoe. They are often promoted into management because they were good workers in their previous position, but have they been trained to be managers? Many times, the answer is unfortunately NO. That's why new managers often have a really hard time with delegation – they're simply used to doing the work themselves. But as new managers, continuing to do so will mean sure failure, which is why so many new managers do in fact end up failing. The great thing about this book is that traces the lived experience of 19 different managers in their first year, and it wasn't easy for any of them. Making the transition from worker to manager is a huge psychological leap. By the end of the book, you'll have a great understanding of being a manager and a leader.

- Himsel, D., *Leadership Sopranos Style: How to Become a More Effective Boss.* Dearborn Trade, 2003. Conflicting loyalties. This one is such a great concept. The huge changes that faced the Soprano family in their rapidly evolving landscape mirror the same kinds of huge changes that modern businesses face on a daily basis. There's a lot of lessons to be learned in the comparison, and this book brings them out in spades.

- Hunter, J., *World's Most Powerful Leadership Principle: How to Become a Servant Leader.* Crown Publishing, 2004. I love the juxtaposition presented in the title of this book – the idea that the most *powerful* leadership principle in the world might be that of being a *servant!* It kind of turns things upside down, but in a really good way. Hunter says that leadership and character development are the exact same thing. But we all know how hard it is to change ourselves. Still, that is the work of the servant leader. His ideas are definitely game-changers, even though they're quite simple.

- Isaacs, W., *Dialogue: The Art of Thinking Together.* Currency/Doubleday, 1999. This is another book on the importance of communication in the form of dialog. There's simply no effective substitute for learning how to be in open and honest conversation with others as a way to strengthen relationships and do what needs to be done in the workplace.

- Josefowitz, N., *You're The Boss! A Guide to Managing a Diverse Work Force with Understanding and Effectiveness.* Warner Books, 1985. This is another great book for anyone who's on the verge of becoming a manager and feels a bit intimidated by the whole idea. There's a lot happening in making this transition, and this book helps you through it so you can be an effective manager of all kinds of people, including the art of dealing with your own stress!

- Kouzes, J. & Posner, B., *The Leadership Challenge, 3rd Edition.* Jossey-Bass, 2002. This book has been around since 1987 and it's become a hugely important work people all around the world. What's interesting is that they maintain that the fundamentals of leadership have remained unchanged over those years (and all of history for that matter). What has changed is the context, which is an important contribution of this book.

- Kouzes, J. & Posner, B., *A Leader's Legacy.* Jossey-Bass Management Series, 2006. As a leader, you want to have a lasting impact on your organization, which is what is meant by the word *legacy.* In this book, the authors take a deep look at what you should pay attention to if you're concerned about the legacy you leave behind when your leadership journey comes to an end.

- Kouzes, J. & Posner, B., *Credibility: How Leaders Can Gain and Lose It, and Why People Demand It.* Jossey-Bass, 2011. Do you have credibility as a leader? Make no mistake, you *need* it, and others will demand it of you. So how do you get it and keep it? The authors argue persuasively that it's all about *relationships*, which should come as no surprise. First published in 1993, this is a fully revised version with a lot of new and important case studies and lots of updated research. The authors go into detail about six key practices that lead to greater credibility if done consistently and done well.

- Kouzes, J. & Posner, B., *Encouraging the Heart: A Leader's Guide to Rewarding and Recognizing Others.* Jossey-Bass, 2003. These authors are definitely among the kings of leadership experts, which is why I'm including a fourth book from them. This one is all about encouragement, and you know I'm really big on that concept myself. Making sure you recognize people's accomplishments is extremely important. So is maintaining mutual respect throughout your organization. It all comes down to helping people realize and fulfill their roles in ways that make them feel like true heroes. And isn't that what you want all your people to feel like?

- Krisco, K., *Leadership & the Art of Conversation.* Prima, 1997. Yes, another book on conversation, because it's just so important to being and effective director, supervisor, manager, or leader. There's lots of talk and chat that happens in the workplace, but how much of it is really and truly *communication?* Very little, I'm afraid to say. By changing the way we talk, we can transform ourselves into great managers and leaders.

- Lawson, K., *Successful Assertive Management*. Barron's Educational Series, 2006. As a director, you have to know the art of being assertive or you're dead in the water. This practical book offers you great ways to make sure you know how to motivate your staff to do what needs to be done to make the organization more successful. Whether it's being clear in your communication or learning how to optimize matching people and tasks, this book has the strategies and tactics you need to make it happen.

- Lawson, K., *Success in Dealing With Difficult People*. Barron's Educational Series, 2006. You will inevitably have to deal with difficult people in the workplace, so why not take the time to learn how to deal with them effectively? This book offers a series of simple things to keep in mind when dealing with difficult people that will make those interactions more productive and get better results.

- Leeds, D., *Smart Questions: The Essential Strategy for Successful Managers*. Berkeley Business, 1987. All too often people rush to provide answers – in part because our educational system values answers more than questions, but asking great questions is an absolute necessity for anyone who wants to be a good manager. This book shows you how to do it.

- Lundin, S., Paul, H., & Christensen J., *Fish! A Remarkable Way to Boost Morale and Improve Results*. Hyperion, 2000. It may be hard to imagine your organization being one where everyone comes to work each day full of passion and energy to do their very best, but it can happen. This book is presented as a fictional parable in which a manager is charged with transforming an organization to embody better attitudes. The manager draws upon what she sees in the fish market across the street to accomplish her task.

- Maxwell, J.C., *The 21 Indispensable Qualities of a Leader: Becoming the Person Others Will Want to Follow.* Thomas Nelson Publishers, 1999. Maxwell is a giant in the fields of leadership and management, known best for his classic bestselling book, *The 21 Irrefutable laws of Leadership.* This great book on leadership offers a concise look at the 21 qualities that make for great leaders, along with help in applying it in your own leadership life.

- Maxwell, J. C., *The 17 Indisputable Laws of Teamwork: Embrace Them and Empower Your Team.* Thomas Nelson, 2013 (reprint edition). Maxwell's book on building successful teams is a must-read. He has come up with 17 points that each deserves careful consideration. We're talking here about things like the *law of high morale,* the *law of the Big Picture,* the *law of the Scoreboard,* and the *Law of the Price Tag,* to name just a few. Intrigued? You should be!

- McGinty, S.M., *Power Talk: Using Language to Build Authority and Influence.* Warner Books, 2001. This book highlights the importance of oral communication to success in the workplace. Yes, you can actually talk your way up the corporate ladder if you pay close attention to the advice offered in this book. It's all about making sure you use the right speaking style for the situation you're in at the moment. If you need to be heard, this is the book for you.

- Miller, J.B., *Best Boss-Worst Boss: Lessons and Laughs from the International Best Boss/Worst Boss Contest.* Fireside Books, 1996. Often humorous, this one is worth the read once again to see if you might recognize yourself in any of these stories about best and worst bosses. The author comes up with all kinds of different archetypal models for different kinds of bosses, like the contrast between Santa and Scrooge, or the differences between dictators and humanitarians. Which sides of these equations will you be on?

- Miller, L.E. & Miller, J., *A Woman's Guide to Successful Negotiating: How to Convince, Collaborate, & Create Your Way to Agreement (2nd Edition)*. McGraw Hill, 2010. Women often feel like they aren't good at negotiating, but that's because they're often comparing themselves to how men do it. There are kinds of mistakes that women make when try to negotiate, and this book helps women become aware of them, how to avoid them, and how to engage in effective negotiating techniques. Women can be effective negotiators, and this books shows how to do it.

- Mindell, P., *How to Say It for Women: Communicating with Confidence and Power; Using the Language of Success*. Prentice-Hall, 2003. This is another book aimed at women to help them take on the language of success, which may feel somewhat foreign to them at first. It's time to ditch the typically weak phrases and replace them with the ones that display authority and confidence to get things done.

- Mindell, P., *How to Say It for Executives: The Complete Guide to Communication for Leaders*. Prentice-Hall, 2005. This version of Mindell's book is not gender-specific, but aimed at executives and leaders in general. From major speeches to routine daily interactions, this book gives you the language and skills to talk in ways that get your ideas across clearly and effectively.

- Mitchell, J., *Hug Your People: The Proven Way to Hire, Inspire, and Recognize Your Employees and Achieve Remarkable Results*. Hachette Books, 2008. This book is all about how to keep your most important asset, your people, happy and thriving in your organization. You've got to treat people in a way that builds trust and makes them proud to be working for your organization. If you can create a culture of niceness, you'll be way ahead of the curve. Each chapter also has a handy checklist that summarizes important points. There are all kinds of subtle changes you can make that will transform your organization in positive ways.

- O'Brien, P., *Positive Management: Assertiveness for Managers*. Nicholas Brealey Publishing, 1992. Being both assertive and positive is a winning combination that allows you to defuse tense situations, even when they are super-charge with emotion. This is a great skill set to develop as a director or supervisor.

- O'Connor, C.A., *Successful Leadership*. Barron's, 1997. It took a long time before people realized that leaders don't have to be born to be leaders – many of the skills and practices needed to become an effective leader can be learned and developed. You need to realistically assess your starting point, however, to know how much work lies ahead for you as an aspiring leader.

- Pollan, S.M. & Levine, M., Eds., *Life Scripts for Managers: What to Say to Get What You Want in 101 of Life's Toughest Situations*. Macmillan, 1999. Many of the toughest situations you face seem hopeless because you just don't have the words you need to address them. But these are things you can learn. In fact, why not script out what words you need in certain situations? That's exactly what this book does. It not only gives you the words you need, but also lots of advice on how to deliver them.

- Runion, M., *Perfect Phrases for Managers & Supervisors: Hundreds of Ready-to-Use Phrases for Any Management Situation*. McGraw-Hill, 2004. This is another book full of ready-made phrases that can be used in a wide variety of managerial situations, and it's especially geared towards those who are relatively new or are at the middle level. Once again it also includes plenty of tips for effective delivery. And just as important as what you need to say is what *not* to say, which is also covered in this valuable resource.

- Ruskin, M., *Speaking Up: What to Say to Your Boss and Everyone Else Who Gets on Your Case*. Bob Adams Publishers, 1997. We've all be victims of failing to deliver the perfect comeback, right? I don't know about you, but it's often several hours or several days later that I come up with the response I wish I had given in whatever situation. This is all about holding your ground when you're feeling overwhelmed or intimidated by others so you can still deliver that perfect comeback that gets the results you want. If you're looking to put words to work for you, this is an important book to read.

- Scholtes, P., *The Leader's Handbook: A Guide to Inspiring Your People and Managing the Daily Workflow*. As managers it's all too easy to start blaming others for problems in the workplace. What this book does is help you get past the blame game so you can figure out what's really going wrong and fix it. Many times, it's the *system* that needs fixing, not your workers! Rather than pointing fingers at people, this books shows you how to roll up your sleeves and make real improvements to your work processes.

- Sirota, D., Mischkind, L., & Meltzer, M., *The Enthusiastic Employee: How Companies Profit by Giving Workers What They Want*. Wharton School, 2005. Can you imagine your workplace filled with employees who are downright *enthusiastic* about their jobs? If that seems like a whimsical dream that could never come true, you owe it to yourself to read this book. The idea is that what workers want hasn't really change at all over the years, and it's actually surprisingly easy to give them what they want – fair and equal treatment (which includes adequate compensation and benefits), work that they can feel good about doing, and camaraderie with coworkers. Simple, right? Actually it is. We make it a lot more complicated than it needs to be. The nice thing about this book is that it's backed up very solidly with decades of research, and it's not rocket science!

- Solomon, M., *"What Do I Say When..."* Prentice-Hall, 1988. Here's another book with all kinds of useful phrases that will help you say what needs to be said in particular situations. You can use these to become more successful at work, and to get others to help you with what needs to be accomplished.

- Solomon, M., *Working With Difficult People.* Prentice Hall, 1990. There are all kinds of different types of difficult people that can make your work life miserable. Don't you wish you knew how to deal with them more effectively? That's the topic of this book, and it gives you plenty of tips and strategies that will guide you in your interactions with difficult people.

- Stone, D., Patton, B., & Heen, S., *Difficult Conversations: How to Discuss What Matters Most.* Viking, 1999. Avoiding difficult conversations is kind of like the concept of repression in psychology. You can repress or suppress your strong feelings, but they don't go away, they just keep simmering and then might literally explode in ways that aren't helpful to anyone, yourself included. Avoiding difficult conversations doesn't make their cause go away. It only delays the inevitable, and makes it worse when the confrontation finally happens. This book gives you a step-by-step process for approaching and engaging in those difficult conversations you know you need to have but just can't seem to find the will to do it. Avoidance doesn't work!

- Stumpf, S.A. & DeLuca, J. R., *Learning to Use What You Already Know.* Berrett-Koehler, 1994. Rather than saying "Gosh, I can't do that" or "I don't know how to deal with that." What would happen if you just assumed you already know more than you might think? This book helps you make the connection between what you already know and the situation you're currently dealing with.

- Tannen, D., *You Just Don't Understand: Women & Men in Conversation.* Ballentine Books, 1991. Yes, another book on communication between men and women because it just causes so many problems in organizations. The gender differences are real, but they don't have to result in conflict or paralysis as they so often do. After reading this book, you'll have a much better understanding of how it is that a woman and man can have entirely different impressions of the exact same interaction. It will totally transform how you approach conversations with members of the opposite sex.

- Terry, R., *Authentic Leadership: Courage in Action.* Jossey-Bass, 1993. Another book on authenticity is always a good thing, because we are so in need of greater authenticity in our organizations today. In the midst of tumultuous and rapid change, this books makes you pause and consider what it is we really mean by leadership and what it's for. We need to be crystal clear on those items before we can be effective leaders.

- Wheatley, M., *Finding Our Way: Leadership for an Uncertain Time.* Berrett-Kohler, 2005. Margaret Wheatley is one of the best organization thinkers we have on the entire planet, and this is one of her best books focused on leadership. She brings a lot insights into her work from science (especially quantum physics, chaos theory, and systems thinking) and tends to view organizations like living systems in nature. This book will challenge you to think very differently about your organization, and for the better.

- Wheeler, M., *Problem People at Work.* St. Martin's-Griffin, 1995. Personally, I don't think you can ever read enough books on how to deal with difficult people in the workplace. It's what sucks up most of a director's time, so the more you can learn about it the better off you'll be, right? This one has lots of true-to-life examples that will give you new insights into dealing with problem people at work.

About the Author

Vernon Mason has been an early childhood administrator for over 24 years with a master's degree in Early Childhood Administration from National Louis University. With a $5,000 credit card in 1991 he and his mother opened a small child care center with a capacity of 30 that grew to 125. In 1999 it was destroyed by a natural disaster.

After rebuilding and starting over in just two years, Vernon grew WEE SCHOOL Child Development Center to 248 children. When he turned 40 he purchased 3 troubled childcare centers in just 12 months. What a midlife crisis! He is the owner of four centers with 85 staff caring for 500 children.

As a natural next step several years ago, Vernon began consulting, training, secret-shopping, and giving keynote addresses. He has become known for his inspiring storytelling, candor, and humor in his presentations at local, state, and national conferences. Vernon's popular keynotes and trainings come from real life experiences. He has been hands-on in childcare programs for decades. While being a director he was also a cook, filled-in as needed in classrooms, took care of maintenance (an expert at unclogging toilets), and managed multiple sites.

His keynotes have been described as "exactly what I needed" and "fall down funny." His stories range from doing CPR on a hamster to firing an employee in the middle of Wal-Mart because she felt like shopping instead of working. The stories are unbelievable, real, and remind you that *you're* not crazy, it's everybody else! Some of his most requested keynotes and trainings are Don't Waste a Crisis, where there's a will there's a way, a story of perseverance in tough times; Avoiding Burnout by Finding and Keeping your Happiness; Tackling Turnover, praising and rewarding staff for little or no cost; Zero to Hero, improving an employee's performance or setting them free and Early Childhood/Preschool Classroom Management.

In 2015 Vernon launched Directors Leadership Solutions out of his desire to make directors' paths to success easier. The website is a hub for Vernon to share information he has learned along the way. You will find a variety of resources such as parent communication, dealing with everything from biting, staff turnover, and tuition rate increases, tips on to how to handle parent complaints, getting employees to do what you ask, and developing a healthy work environment. Directors Leadership Solutions is also where businesses and organizations large and small find information on scheduling Vernon for speaking engagements, secret shopping, and to talk administrators through difficult times.

Find Vernon online at the following websites:

http://myweeschool.com

http://directorsleadershipsolutions.com

http://facebook.com/vernon.mason

A Cause That is Close to My Heart!

It had been a rough few years: My partner, Andy, had lost his Mom, Dad, and Brother within a three-year period. Also during that time we lost three more loved ones: Whealton, our 125-pound, fun-loving, gentle giant of a black Labrador; Pepper, a small, high-strung, energetic, happy-to-be-alive 70-pound Dalmatian; and Boots, a very formal tuxedo cat. They were all rescues and lived long, full lives. The loss was palpable because it all came so fast, and we weren't even able to recover from one loss before we experienced yet another.

We had made an agreement not to adopt another dog for at least nine months or a year. In the meantime we did do some doggie transportation. Dogs are transported when a shelter gets full and they need to be moved to foster care to avoid euthanasia. Most are placed in temporary foster care to be kept safe until they can be adopted.

On that Saturday we had transported more than a dozen dogs in my SUV from Rocky Mount, North Carolina, to Richmond, Virginia. It was uneventful and we needed to return the dog crates to the rescue group in Rocky Mount, which happened to be hosting an adoption event called "Paws in the Park." Before going in, Andy said to me, "Don't make eye contact, talk to, or pet any dogs."

We walked up to the rescue group's tent and there was a small pen in the middle with a dozen dogs in various stages of excitement. Of course, I immediately picked up a black poodle named Tonya and Andy picked up a blonde Shih Tzu named Sandy. Well, so much for the pact to not interact with the dogs!

I knew quickly that Tonya was not for me because her excitement level was more than I could handle. Sandy looked at Andy when he picked her up and she laid her head on his arm and exhaled deeply as if to say, "Finally." To make a long story short, we decided *not* to adopt Sandy that day. We stuck to our word and left empty-handed. For over a month we talked about Sandy every day and Andy even renamed her Pickles. There's another whole story about how I kind of accidentally adopted Sandy without Andy knowing!

Ultimately, Pickles came along at the perfect time. There was so much sorrow in our lives, and then there's Pickles demanding that you love her. Pickles came from a puppy mill that was subsequently shut down. She had spent 10 horrific years living in a kennel, birthing an unknown number of litters. Her "caretakers" were polite enough to take the water hose to her and her kennel almost weekly. And yes, she was still in the kennel when they sprayed it and her down.

She was the kind of dog you see on TV that has never seen grass, and to this day she still struggles with some tasks, such as going up steps. She has never been able to go down steps. Pickles is so resilient because even after the neglect and suffering, she manages to love and trust again. She brings us such joy!

As I write this Pickles is sleeping and snoring in one of her favorite places next to my desk. I love that she's become so demanding, and she deserves everything she gets! She birthed countless litters, and because of her pedigree people bought her puppies not realizing they were supporting a puppy mill or her continued inhumane living conditions!

The owners of the mill would clean her up and take her in the house for showings and then toss her back into the kennel when they were done. People have said some very rough things about what should be done to Pickle's previous owners. I explain it like this: They saw Pickles as a commodity, like some farmer's might view a cow or a pig, and to them she was livestock. This does not excuse their behavior, but it does help me to see why they did what they did.

Our beloved Pickles

The ONLY way to stop this kind of behavior is to stop the demand for these puppies. If people would not buy these puppies, then there would be no need for puppy mills.

That's why I say know your breeder, or better yet, ADOPT FROM A LOCAL PET RESCUDE GROUP! If you want a specific breed, go to petfinder.com and adopt!

Made in the USA
Middletown, DE
04 November 2017